Author: Mary Moore

Proofreaders: Alison Hennell, Kieran Maguire

Content Review: Alison Hennell, Kieran Maguire

Editors: Kieran Maguire, Aasha Shamsuddin

Special thanks to John Pinedo who wrote the Financial Instruments and Hedge Accounting chapters

Published by Adkins & Matchett (UK) Limited – trading as Adkins Matchett & Toy

Fourth edition 2012

UK COPYRIGHT NOTICE

Visit us at or buy online: www.amttraining.com

GW00686162

AdkinsMatchett&Toy

AMTM1864

Table of contents

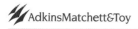

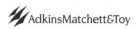
Consolidation and noncontrolling interests

What is a group?

A group is a business and all the other businesses under its control. For example:

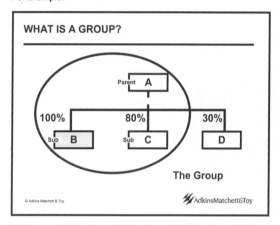

In this example, business A is the "parent" and has invested in businesses B, C and D by buying their equity: 100% in the case of B; 80% in the case of C; and only 30% of D. Companies B and C are different to D because they are **controlled** by A. **Therefore A, B and C are part of the group.**

What about company D? Why are B and C part of the group but not D?

We need to identify the businesses which are controlled by A, and in this case the only information we have to help with this decision is the percentage owned. In straightforward cases, a business must own a majority of the equity in another business in order to gain control. Applying this logic to this example indicates that D is not controlled and is therefore not part of the group. We will deal with the accounting for businesses like D in the next chapter.

The detailed rules on achieving control vary from country to country. However, in most cases, the percentage of the equity owned is the key identifier of a subsidiary. There are situations where this is not the case, but they are outside the scope of this chapter.

So what?

A group of companies must produce a set of accounts as if they were a single trading entity. These accounts are called **consolidated** accounts. Groups are very common and in most cases when you are looking at a set of financial statements they are actually consolidated accounts representing all the activities of the group. It is important to have an understanding of how these consolidated accounts are constructed.

Consolidated or group accounts

Consolidated or group accounts are the financial statements of a parent and all the businesses it controls (its subsidiaries).

There are two main methodologies for consolidating the accounts:

Consolidation! Purchase or pooling?

Pooling is very rare and banned under US GAAP and IFRS. Purchase is the common method

- Pooling or merger method
- Purchase or acquisition method

Pooling is not allowed under US GAAP and IFRS and is very restricted in other parts of the world. The purchase or acquisition method is widespread and is by far the most commonly used methodology.

Pooling or merger method - when to use it

Pooling cannot be used under US GAAP and IFRS. In some countries it may still be used when the deal meets certain very strict criteria. This methodology is intended for situations where two businesses decide to do business together. No party has "purchased" the other. To facilitate this, each of the two groups of shareholders needs to reorganize their shares so that everyone owns shares in the same entity. This will always involve them swapping their existing shares for new shares (normally, newly issued). *These situations are rare in reality since one party to the deal is normally dominant and is actually "buying" the other.*

The rules vary from country to country but they generally specify that:

- It must be a share-for-share exchange
- Most (> 90%) of the shareholders must agree
- No party must be seen as "the buyer"

Pooling or merger method - how to do it

The pooling methodology is easy; *you simply add each line item together*. Even when doing the income statement in the year of the deal, you simply add each line item. *The date of the deal is irrelevant*.

Let's do an example:

Fulton Inc - consolidation using the pooling method!

Fulton and Bristol decide to do business together and merge their businesses. In order to facilitate this deal, it was agreed that the shareholders of Bristol would swap their shares in return for ten new shares issued by Fulton. At the date of the deal Fulton's shares are valued at 25 each.

This means that post-deal, all the shareholders of both businesses now own shares in Fulton. And Fulton owns the shares of Bristol because the shareholders of Bristol paid for their new shares (issued by Fulton) with their Bristol shares instead of with cash.

The balance sheets of both businesses are as follows:

	Fulton	Bristol
Cash	20	10
Receivables	140	70
PP&E	100	60
Goodwill	10	0
Total assets	**270**	**140**
Payables	60	40
Long-term debt	100	20
Capital	65	50
Retained earnings	45	30
Total L and E	**270**	**140**

To do the consolidation using pooling, we simply *add them up*.

	Fulton	Bristol	Combo
Cash	20	10	30
Receivables	140	70	210
PP&E	100	60	160
Goodwill	10	0	10
Total assets	**270**	**140**	**410**
Payables	60	40	100
Long-term debt	100	20	120
Capital	65	50	115
Retained earnings	45	30	75
Total L and E	**270**	**140**	**410**

The combined income statement / profit and loss account can be built using the same procedure. We simply *add* both income statements up. Even in the year of the deal, we ignore the date of the deal and add the income statement / profit and loss account for the whole year.

However, when using the pooling methodology, all published numbers prior to the deal must be restated as if the newly merged entity had always existed.

Purchase or acquisition method - when to use it

This is used for any situation when a business has *control* of another. It is not used when the conditions for using pooling apply. It is by far the most common methodology used worldwide and it is now the only method used under US GAAP and IFRS.

Purchase or acquisition method - the issues

This methodology is more detailed and is driven by two important considerations:

1. One group of shareholders have been bought out; and
2. The buyer almost always has to pay a premium to achieve this.

The first of these points is reflected in the accounting by removing the subsidiaries shareholders' equity from the consolidated numbers. This is always the case. *The shareholders' equity of the subsidiary that existed at the deal date is never included in consolidated shareholders' equity.*

The second issue, the premium paid, is more involved. The most common terminology used to describe this premium is goodwill. Before we consider this in detail, let us talk through an example in order to consider the issues:

Anderlind Inc - so what's goodwill then?

Anderlind has bought 100% of another company for 100,000. The net assets (assets less liabilities) on the balance sheet of the target company at the date of the deal amounted to 75,000. This implies that Anderlind has paid a premium of 25,000. This 25,000 is normally called goodwill. But is it really goodwill?

Let's say that we know that included in the net assets is a property with a book value (value in the balance sheet) of 8,000 but with a real or "fair" value of 13,000. This means that the premium paid above net assets can be broken down into two elements: 5,000 for the unrecorded value of the property (13,000 - 8,000) and only 20,000 for goodwill.

So to calculate goodwill correctly, there are a number of steps we must take:

1. Make adjustments to the target's net assets so that they reflect fair value.
2. Compare that, with the purchase price (also at fair value).

So the goodwill calculation looks like this:

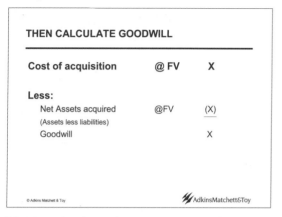

What do you do with goodwill once you have calculated it? In many countries it is amortized over its life. Under US GAAP and IFRS, the goodwill is shown on the balance sheet as a long-term asset and its value is checked regularly. If the value is found to be below that on the balance sheet then it is "written down". This is done by decreasing the goodwill asset and also decreasing retained earnings. This "write down" will be shown as an expense / cost in the income statement / profit and loss account for that year. This process is called "impairment testing".

Purchase or acquisition method - the balance sheet

How do we build the combined balance sheet using the purchase or acquisition method? Here are the steps:

1. Revalue (to fair value) the assets and liabilities of the subsidiary at the deal date.
2. Calculate goodwill.
3. Add each asset and liability line item making sure to include the sub's fair value adjustments.
4. Include the deal goodwill in the combo balance sheet.
5. Record the components of the purchase price.
6. Zap (zero-out) the shareholders' equity of the subsidiary at the deal date.
7. Add everything up.

For example:

Fulton Inc - the purchase method!

This is the same example as above but using the purchase method. Remember Fulton issued 10 new shares and their market value was $25 each. Fulton has not yet recorded this share issue. Here are the balance sheets with the fair values for Bristol.

STEP 1 - revalue Bristol's assets and liabilities

	Fulton	Bristol	FV Bristol
Cash	20	10	10
Receivables	140	70	50
PP&E	100	60	100
Goodwill	10	0	0
Total assets	**270**	**140**	
Payables	60	40	40
Long-term debt	100	20	20
Capital	65	50	
Retained earnings	45	30	
Total L and E	**270**	**140**	

STEP 2 - calculate the goodwill

What you paid	250
(10 * 25)	
Net assets bought	80
(140 - 40 - 20) * 100%	
Revaluation adjustment	20
(50 - 70) + (100 - 60)	

So:

Acquisition price @ FV	250
Less: Net assets bought @ FV	(100)
Goodwill	**150**

STEP 3 - add the assets / liabilities including revaluation adjustments of subsidiary

	Fulton	Bristol	FV Bristol	Combo
Cash	20	10	10	30
Receivables	140	70	50	190
PP&E	100	60	100	200
Goodwill	10	0	0	
Total assets	**270**	**140**		
Payables	60	40	40	100
Long-term debt	100	20	20	120
Capital	65	50		
Retained earnings	45	30		
Total L and E	**270**	**140**		

STEP 4 - include the deal goodwill

	Fulton	Bristol	FV Bristol	Adj.	Combo
Cash	20	10	10		30
Receivables	140	70	50		190
PP&E	100	60	100		200
Goodwill	10	0	0	150	160
Total assets	**270**	**140**			
Payables	60	40	40		100
Long-term debt	100	20	20		120
Capital	65	50			
Retained earnings	45	30			
Total L and E	**270**	**140**			

STEP 5 - include the components of purchase price

	Fulton	Bristol	FV Bristol	Adj.	Combo
Cash	20	10	10		30
Receivables	140	70	50		190
PP&E	100	60	100		200
Goodwill	10	0	0	150	160
Total assets	**270**	**140**			
Payables	60	40	40		100
Long-term debt	100	20	20		120
Capital	65	50		250	
Retained earnings	45	30			
Total L and E	**270**	**140**			

STEP 6 - zap out the sub's shareholders' equity at deal date

	Fulton	Bristol	FV Bristol	Adj.	Combo
Cash	20	10	10		30
Receivables	140	70	50		190
PP&E	100	60	100		200
Goodwill	10	0	0	150	160
Total assets	**270**	**140**			**580**
Payables	60	40	40		100
Long-term debt	100	20	20		120
Capital	65	50		250 (50)	315
Retained earnings	45	30		(30)	45
Total L and E	**270**	**140**			**580**

And it balances!

In summary

Fundamentally what we are doing can be summarized as follows:

In summary!

Buyer +
Target + / -
Deal changes =
Consolidated

Buyer + Target + / - Deal changes = Consolidated numbers

So the trick is to understand what the deal changes are. They are likely to include some if not all of the following:

■ Asset or liability fair value changes (step-ups or step-downs)
■ Deal goodwill
■ Deal financing
■ Zero out the shareholders' equity of the target

Purchase or acquisition method - the income statement / profit and loss account

Simply add everything together line-by-line. Include deal amortization if goodwill is being amortized (remember, goodwill is not amortized under US GAAP or IFRS). In the year of the deal, include the income statement / profit and loss account of the subsidiary from the deal date only.

Just as for the balance sheet, this can easily be summarized as

In summary!

Buyer +
Target + / -
Deal changes =
Consolidated

Buyer + Target + / - Deal changes = Consolidated numbers

So the trick is to understand what the deal changes are. They are likely to include some if not all of the following:

■ Implications of asset or liability fair value changes (extra depreciation on a PP&E step-up for example)
■ Synergies assumed
■ Deal financing impact (extra interest on new debt)
■ Tax implications of the above changes

Purchase or acquisition method - the cash flow statement

Build it in exactly the same way as for a single entity but use the consolidated balance sheets and income statement / profit and loss accounts.

Purchase or acquisition method - some other details

Inter-company items

ALL ...... on consolidation!

Consolidated accounts show the financial performance of a group of businesses as if they were a single trading entity. It would be very easy to achieve sales growth by getting the businesses to trade with each other. To stop this happening there is a general rule for consolidated accounts which says:

All inter-group trading and balances must be cancelled on consolidation

Khaku Inc - inter-group balances and trading!

Khaku Inc has a subsidiary called Nasheela and they trade with each other. During the year Nasheela sold products to Khaku for $135,000 and at the year-end Khaku owed Nasheela $13,700 in respect of this trading.

Extracts from the financial statements are as follows. Calculate the consolidated numbers assuming no other adjustments are necessary to these line items.

	Khaku	Nasheela
Sales	1,988,765	1,350,000
COGS	1,034,158	648,000
Gross Profit	954,607	702,000
Receivables	288,844	140,550
Payables	155,832	88,760

	Khaku	Nasheela	Adj.	Combo
Sales	1,988,765	1,350,000	(135,000)	3,203,765
COGS	1,034,158	648,000	(135,000)	1,547,158
Gross Profit	954,607	702,000		1,656,607
Receivables	288,844	140,550	(13,700)	415,694
Payables	155,832	88,760	(13,700)	230,892

Noncontrolling shareholders

Who are they?

Noncontrolling shareholders!

They own a part of one of the subsidiaries

Noncontrolling shareholders (historically known as minority shareholders or minority interests) exist when the parent controls a subsidiary but does not own all of the equity of that business. In this case some of the equity funding of the group is provided by shareholders other that those who own the parent. *Noncontrolling shareholders own a share of part of the group.* This cannot be ignored.

So how do we deal with them?

We consolidate 100% all of the net assets and all of the income statement / profit and loss account as normal but:

■ We include an extra line in the liability and equity section of the balance sheet called *noncontrolling interest.*

This is calculated in two possible ways depending on which GAAP is being followed.

Under IFRS, choose either

■ Noncontrolling shareholders' % **of fair value of the shareholders' equity** of the relevant subsidiary (called **shareholder equity method** from now on)

This is straightforward to calculate.

or

■ **Fair value** of the noncontrolling interest (called **fair value method** from now on)

The fair value of the noncontrolling interest under the fair value method can be based on the share price, if there is one, or another valuation method such as trading comparables analysis. It should reflect a minority discount compared to the fair value per share of a controlling interest. The selected valuation method needs to be disclosed in the financial statements. This fair value exercise only occurs on the acquisition of the controlling interest by the parent. There is no need to record any subsequent changes in the fair value of the NCI.

Under US GAAP, the only acceptable method for noncontrolling interest in the balance sheet is the **fair value method**.

■ We include an extra line at the bottom of the income statement / profit and loss account called *noncontrolling interest*. This is calculated by taking their % of the net income / profit after tax of the relevant subsidiary.

Goodwill and noncontrolling interests

Using the fair value method for noncontrolling interests means that they will be allocated a share of goodwill. Let's look at some examples.

Peder Inc - noncontrolling interests in the balance sheet, at % of fair value of shareholders' equity

Peder bought 90% of Fenland for 500 in a cash deal. At the date of the deal, the fair value of Fenland was equal to the book value (so no revaluation adjustments are necessary). Today, the balance sheets of both businesses are as follows:

	Peder	Fenland
Cash	820	210
Receivables	540	670
PP&E	900	960
Goodwill	10	0
Total assets	**2,270**	**1,840**
Payables	660	540
Long-term debt	800	820
Capital	465	50
Retained earnings	345	430
Total L and E	**2,270**	**1,840**

Remember the steps:

We need to add an extra step for the noncontrolling interest calculation.

STEP 1 - revalue Fenland's assets and liabilities

In this case fair value is equal to book value so nothing to do.

STEP 2 - calculate the goodwill

Acquisition price @ FV	500
Less: Net assets bought @ FV	(432)
(1,840 - 540 - 820) * 90%	
Goodwill on Peder's stake in Fenland	**68**
Goodwill on NCI stake in Fenland	**0**
Deal goodwill	**68**

STEP 3 - add the assets / liabilities including revaluation adjustments of subsidiary

	Peder	Fenland	Adj.	Combo
Cash	820	210		1,030
Receivables	540	670		1,210
PP&E	900	960		1,860
Goodwill	10	0		
Total assets	**2,270**	**1,840**		
Payables	660	540		1,200
Long-term debt	800	820		1,620
Capital	465	50		
Retained earnings	345	430		
Total L and E	**2,270**	**1,840**		

STEP 4 - include the deal goodwill

	Peder	Fenland	Adj.	Combo
Cash	820	210		1,030
Receivables	540	670		1,210
PP&E	900	960		1,860
Goodwill	10	0	68	78
Total assets	**2,270**	**1,840**		
Payables	660	540		1,200
Long-term debt	800	820		1,620
Capital	465	50		
Retained earnings	345	430		
Total L and E	**2,270**	**1,840**		

STEP 5 - calculate and include the noncontrolling interest

Noncontrolling interest   48
(50 + 430) * 10%

	Peder	Fenland	Adj.	Combo
Cash	820	210		1,030
Receivables	540	670		1,210
PP&E	900	960		1,860
Goodwill	10	0	68	78
Total assets	**2,270**	**1,840**		
Payables	660	540		1,200
Long-term debt	800	820		1,620
Capital	465	50		
Retained earnings	345	430		
Noncontrolling interests	0	0	**48**	48
Total L and E	**2,270**	**1,840**		

STEP 6 - include the components of purchase price

	Peder	Fenland	Adj.	Combo
Cash	820	210	**(500)**	530
Receivables	540	670		1,210
PP&E	900	960		1,860
Goodwill	10	0	68	78
Total assets	**2,270**	**1,840**		
Payables	660	540		1,200
Long-term debt	800	820		1,620
Capital	465	50		
Retained earnings	345	430		
Noncontrolling interests	0	0	48	48
Total L and E	**2,270**	**1,840**		

STEP 7 - zap out the sub's shareholders' equity at deal date

	Peder	Fenland	Adj.	Combo
Cash	820	210	**(500)**	530
Receivables	540	670		1,210
PP&E	900	960		1,860
Goodwill	10	0	68	78
Total assets	**2,270**	**1,840**		**3,678**
Payables	660	540		1,200
Long-term debt	800	820		1,620
Capital	465	50	**(50)**	465
Retained earnings	345	430	**(430)**	345
Noncontrolling interests	0	0	48	48
Total L and E	**2,270**	**1,840**		**3,678**

And it balances!

Peder Inc - noncontrolling interests in the balance sheet, at fair value

Peder bought 90% of Fenland for 500 in a cash deal. At the date of the deal, the fair value of Fenland was equal to the book value (so no revaluation adjustments are necessary). **The fair value of the noncontrolling interest has been estimated at 60.** Today, the balance sheets of both businesses are as follows:

	Peder	Fenland
Cash	820	210
Receivables	540	670
PP&E	900	960
Goodwill	10	0
Total assets	**2,270**	**1,840**
Payables	660	540
Long-term debt	800	820
Capital	465	50
Retained earnings	345	430
Noncontrolling interests	0	0
Total L and E	**2,270**	**1,840**

Remember the steps:

We need to add an extra step for the minority interest calculation.

STEP 1 - revalue Fenland's assets and liabilities

In this case fair value is equal to book value so nothing to do.

STEP 2 - calculate the goodwill

Acquisition price @ FV	500
Less: Net assets bought @ FV	(432)
(1,840 - 540 - 820) * 90%	
Goodwill on Peder's stake in Fenland	**68**
Goodwill on NCI stake in Fenland	**12**
(60 - ((1,840 - 540 - 820) * 10%)	
Deal goodwill	**80**

STEP 3 - add the assets / liabilities including revaluation adjustments of subsidiary

	Peder	Fenland	Adj.	Combo
Cash	820	210		1,030
Receivables	540	670		1,210
PP&E	900	960		1,860
Goodwill	10	0		
Total assets	**2,270**	**1,840**		
Payables	660	540		1,200
Long-term debt	800	820		1,620
Capital	465	50		
Retained earnings	345	430		
Total L and E	**2,270**	**1,840**		

STEP 4 - include the deal goodwill

	Peder	Fenland	Adj.	Combo
Cash	820	210		1,030
Receivables	540	670		1,210
PP&E	900	960		1,860
Goodwill	10	0	80	90
Total assets	**2,270**	**1,840**		
Payables	660	540		1,200
Long-term debt	800	820		1,620
Capital	465	50		
Retained earnings	345	430		
Total L and E	**2,270**	**1,840**		

STEP 5 - calculate and include the noncontrolling interest

Noncontrolling interest at fair value   60

	Peder	Fenland	Adj.	Combo
Cash	820	210		1,030
Receivables	540	670		1,210
PP&E	900	960		1,860
Goodwill	10	0	80	90
Total assets	**2,270**	**1,840**		
Payables	660	540		1,200
Long-term debt	800	820		1,620
Capital	465	50		
Retained earnings	345	430		
Noncontrolling interests	0	0	60	60
Total L and E	**2,270**	**1,840**		

STEP 6 - include the components of purchase price

	Peder	Fenland	Adj.	Combo
Cash	820	210	(500)	530
Receivables	540	670		1,210
PP&E	900	960		1,860
Goodwill	10	0	80	90
Total assets	**2,270**	**1,840**		
Payables	660	540		1,200
Long-term debt	800	820		1,620
Capital	465	50		
Retained earnings	345	430		
Noncontrolling interests	0	0	60	60
Total L and E	**2,270**	**1,840**		

STEP 7 - zap out the sub's shareholders' equity at deal date

	Peder	Fenland	Adj	Combo
Cash	820	210	(500)	530
Receivables	540	670		1,210
PP&E	900	960		1,860
Goodwill	10	0	80	90
Total assets	**2,270**	**1,840**		**3,690**
Payables	660	540		1,200
Long-term debt	800	820		1,620
Capital	465	50	(50)	465
Retained earnings	345	430	(430)	345
Noncontrolling interests	0	0	60	60
Total L and E	**2,270**	**1,840**		**3,690**

And it balances!

Peder Inc - noncontrolling interest BASE analysis!

Noncontrolling interests are shareholders and like all shareholders they own shareholders' equity. Shareholders' equity goes up as the business earns profits and goes down as the business pays dividends. Since minority interest is simply a % of shareholders' equity then the minority *BASE* analysis works in the same way.

During the year Peder paid dividends of 30.

	NCI at % of stockholders equity	NCI at fair value
Beginning balance	48	60
Add - % of net income / profit after tax	17	17
Subtract - % of dividends paid	(3)	(3)
Ending balance	62	74

Analyzing noncontrolling interests!

Use a BASE analysis!

Peder Inc - noncontrolling interests and the cash flow statement!

The consolidated cash flow statement is built using the consolidated balance sheets and income statement / profit and loss account. This means that the cash flows of the subsidiary will automatically be included. But there is an extra line item in the balance sheet (and remember the cash flow is a reconciliation of the balance sheet so all balance sheet items must be included).

So let's look at the noncontrolling line in the balance sheet.

From the *BASE* analysis above we can see what causes the change between the beginning and the ending balance sheet number. But we need to decide if these changes are:

- Operating cash flows
- Investing cash flows
- Financing cash flows

Well, we already know that profits are operating and dividends are financing.

So extracts from Peder's consolidated cash flow statement will be as follows:

Operating cash flows

Net income / profit after tax	387
Noncontrolling interest	17

And this 17 is a positive number since it makes noncontrolling interest increase and we know that when a liability and equity item increases the effect on cash is positive.

Financing cash flows

Dividends paid to noncontrolling interests	(3)

This figure is a negative cash flow since it makes noncontrolling interest decrease. When a liability or equity item decreases the effect on cash is negative.

Some more detailed issues

Fees

So how are the deal fees accounted for? In fact it depends upon what kind of fees we are talking about. There are three categories that we need to review:

- Equity issuance fees
- Debt issuance fees
- Advisory fees

Equity issuance fees are deducted from additional paid in capital / share premium account. If we assume they are paid in cash then the following represents the accounting engineering:

Assets	**=**	**Liabilities and Equity**
Cash ↓		APIC ↓

This means that the costs associated with an equity issuance are never reported in the income statement / profit and loss account and therefore never affect net income or earnings per share.

Debt issuance fees are deducted from the debt raised. The accounting engineering looks like this:

Assets	**=**	**Liabilities and Equity**
Cash ↓		Debt ↓

Sometimes, these fees are shown as an asset on the balance sheet

Assets	**=**	**Liabilities and Equity**
Cash ↓		
Prepaid fees ↑		

In both instances the fees are amortized into the income statement / profit and loss account over the life of the debt. This will be reported as part of the interest cost so will impact net income and earnings per share. It will not, however, have any effect on EBIT or EBITDA.

Advisory fees on the other hand are expensed in the first year post deal.

This means that reported operating profit is reduced by the advisory fees. Reported net income is reduced by the advisory fees net of any tax impact. EBIT and EBITDA are unlikely to be impacted since the advisory fees will almost certainly be treated as a non-recurring item. Recurring net income will most likely also be cleaned of the post tax advisory fees.

This means that EBIT, EBITDA, net income and earnings per share are affected, unless they have been cleaned for this "non-recurring" expense. This is a change from the previous accounting treatment of adding them to purchase price, so that they became capitalized as part of goodwill.

Assets	=	**Liabilities and Equity**
Cash ⬇		Retained earnings ⬇

Tax impact of deals

There are several areas which required consideration in respect of the impact on reported taxes. These are covered in the taxes section of this Midnight Manual.

Equity method investments

There are two areas that we must consider when understanding equity method accounting:

- We must explore what an equity method investment or associate actually is
- We need to work out how the accounting works

What is an equity method investment or associate?

An equity method investment / associate is an investment in the equity of another business. However, the owners of these investments are interested in more than just dividend income or capital growth. They have a strategic interest in the operations of the business. Hence, the level of ownership is greater than you would expect from a normal equity investor and less than the level that would achieve overall control. For example:

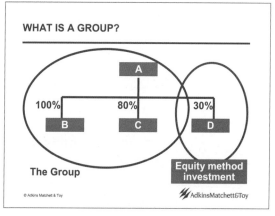

You will recall from the same example in the previous chapter that business A is the "parent" and has invested in businesses B, C and D as a result of buying their equity (100% in the case of B, 80% in the case of C and only 30% of D). A *controls* B and C, but A only owns 30% of D. This would indicate an equity method investment / associate since it is below the level of control but higher than a straightforward equity investment. An ownership level of 20% – 50% is generally considered to be an equity method investment in the absence of information to the contrary. Often in these cases, A will have the right to appoint directors to the board, as well as being involved in both strategic and operational decision making.

**Equity method investments!
What are they?**

Where the parent has significant influence but not control

So what?

Well, a straightforward financial investment in the equity of another is simply included in the balance sheet at cost with dividend income reflected in the income statement / profit and loss account. Capital gains are only reflected when the investment is actually sold. This method of accounting seems inappropriate in the case of equity method investments since it is much more than a financial investment. On the other hand, full consolidation is also inappropriate since this is not a controlled business. We need an "accounting half way house"! Equity method accounting is exactly that. In fact it is often describes as *one line consolidation*.

Equity method accounting

Equity method accounting is used in the consolidated or group accounts for investments that are not controlled but where the parent exerts significant influence. Let's look at the accounting in each of the financial statements in turn.

Equity method accounting and the balance sheet

Equity method investments are shown in a single line item in the long-term assets section of the balance sheet.

This number is made up of *original cost adjusted by changes in equity* each year.

Peder Inc - equity method investments in the balance sheet

Peder bought 30% of Fenland for 160 cash. Produce the consolidated balance sheet for Peder including its investment in Fenland.

	Peder	Fenland
Cash	820	210
Receivables	540	670
PP&E	900	960
Goodwill	10	0
Total assets	**2,270**	**1,840**
Payables	660	540
Long-term debt	800	820
Capital	465	50
Retained earnings	345	430
Total L and E	**2,270**	**1,840**

	Peder	Fenland	Adj.	Combo
Cash	820	210	**(160)**	660
Receivables	540	670		540
PP&E	900	960		900
Goodwill	10	0		10
Equity method investments	0	0	160	160
Total assets	**2,270**	**1,840**		**2,270**
Payables	660	540		660
Long-term debt	800	820		800
Capital	465	50		465
Retained earnings	345	430		345
Total L and E	**2,270**	**1,840**		**2,270**

Equity method accounting!

One line consolidation…

Equity method accounting and the income statement / profit and loss account

Again, this is *one line consolidation*. In this case it is made up of:

% of net income / profit after tax

Peder Inc - equity method investments in the income statement!

The following year the income statements / profit and loss accounts of Peder and Fenland are as follows:

	Peder	Fenland	Combo
Sales	1,785	888	1,785
COGS	982	474	982
Gross profit	803	414	803
SG&A	393	147	393
Operating profit	410	267	410
Interest expense	60	24	60
Equity income	0	0	51
Profit before tax	350	243	401
Tax expense	116	73	116
Net income	**234**	**170**	**285**

% of Net income / profit after tax	51
(170 * 30%)	

Analyzing equity method investments!

Use a *BASE* analysis!

Peder Inc - equity method investments BASE analysis!

We know from basic accounting that shareholders' equity goes up as the business earns profits and goes down as the business pays dividends. The equity method BASE analysis works in the same way.

During the year Fenland paid dividends of 30.

Beginning balance	160
Add - % of net income / profit after tax	51
Subtract - % of dividends paid (30% * 30)	(9)
Ending balance	202

And how does the accounting work here:

Assets	=	**Liabilities and Equity**
Equity inv ↑ 42		Retained earnings ↑ 51
Cash ↑ 9		

Equity method accounting and the cash flow statement

Peder Inc - equity method investments in the cash flow statement

The consolidated cash flow statement is built using the consolidated balance sheets and income statement / profit and loss account. This means that the cash flows of the equity investment will automatically be included. But there is an extra line item in the balance sheet (and remember the cash flow is a reconciliation of the balance sheets so all balance sheet items must be included).

So let's look at the equity method investment line in the balance sheet.

Using the *BASE* analysis above we can see what causes the change between the beginning and the ending balance sheet number. This is an investment and our return is the profits (an operating flow) earned on our behalf, but not all of this return has been received in cash. Only the dividend portion has been received in cash, with the remainder being reinvested in the business. The whole amount of the profit is included in net income, but some of this is not a cash flow and must be removed in the operating section of the cash flow. The *BASE* analysis tells us how much.

Extracts from Peder's consolidated cash flow statement will therefore be as follows:

Operating cash flows

Net income	285 (includes 51)
Equity income less dividends received (51 - 9)	(42)
Operating cash flow	xxx (includes 9)

Taxes

Taxes

Taxes are an expense item like any other albeit one where the calculation of the amount of the expense requires expert knowledge. Once you know the amount of the tax expense, the accounting engineering is straightforward:

Assets	=	**Liabilities and Equity**
Cash ↓		Equity ↓
		(retained earnings goes down as tax expense goes up)

If paid in cash or:

Assets	=	**Liabilities and Equity**
		Taxes payable ↑
		Equity ↓

If paid in arrears.

The most important thing to remember is that the *tax expense* is an accrued number not a cash number. The calculation is done by taking the profits as reported under GAAP and applying the relevant tax rate to those profits. *Taxes payable*, however, is the cash taxes that must be paid to the tax authorities. It is calculated by using the information on the tax return which may or may not be the same as that reported in the income statement / profit and loss account. In most situations, the tax expense number (an accrued number) will not be equal to the taxes that must be paid per the tax return which poses a problem for the engineering shown above. This is solved by using *deferred taxes*.

GAAP numbers versus tax numbers?

Two sets of accounts

The first step in understanding reported taxes is the knowledge that businesses keep two sets of accounts:

- **GAAP accounts** are prepared for shareholders so that they can see how the business is performing
- **TAX accounts** are prepared for the government to calculate how much tax the company has to pay

The differences between GAAP accounts and tax accounts can be divided into two distinctly different types called:

- Permanent differences and
- Temporary differences

Permanent differences

These arise when the rules for reporting under GAAP are different to those for reporting your taxes. The most common version of this kind of difference is when expenses are non-deductible for taxes. For example, in some countries, entertaining expenses are non-deductible for tax purposes. These expenses certainly must be reported under GAAP, probably as part of SG&A but they will be ignored when calculating profits subject to taxes. This means that the taxable profits will be bigger than profits before tax in the income statement / profit and loss account.

In this case, the rules are simply different. This is not something which will "go away" but the effect of this tax rule is that it costs a business more to undertake entertaining as a result. This is adjusted for in the tax expense calculation to recognise the fact that the tax expense is actually economically higher.

These differences are called **permanent differences** and are **adjusted for in the tax expense** calculation as follows:

Tax expense = (Profits before tax + / - permanent differences) * Tax %

Because the tax expense is adjusted, these differences do not cause any variation between tax expense and taxes payable (unlike timing differences below).

Temporary differences

In this case the GAAP numbers and the tax return numbers also differ but only due to the time period in which the item is reported. The underlying treatment is identical in both cases. The most common example of this kind of difference is depreciation. This is often calculated using a straight line basis for GAAP purposes but is nearly always calculated for taxes using an accelerated basis methodology. In both cases the cost of the asset reduces reported profits but the detailed amount period by period will differ. By the end of the life of the asset the amounts deduced against GAAP profits will equal the amounts deduced against taxable profits.

For example:

An asset cost 250 and is expected to have nil residual value at the end of its life. The GAAP policy for depreciation is straight line over 5 years and the tax depreciation profile is over 3 years, 110, 90 and 50 consecutively. You summarize the deductions as follows:

	TAX	GAAP
Year 1	110	50
Year 2	90	50
Year 3	50	50
Year 4	0	50
Year 5	0	50

Sidebar:

Permanent differences

Adjusted in the tax expense calculation
=
(PBT + / - perm. diffs.) * % tax rate

Temporary differences

Adjusted in the balance sheet
=
(Diff.) * % tax rate

Under tax the total deduction over the course of the 5-year period in respect of this asset is the cost of 250 and under GAAP the same comment can be made. In fact the treatment for both taxes and GAAP is identical, but the timing of the treatment differs. This is a classic *temporary difference*. These differences are **adjusted for on the balance sheet** via inclusion of a deferred tax balance to take account of the difference between tax expense, which uses the GAAP numbers for its calculation and taxes payable, which uses the tax numbers as its basis. The deferred tax balance in the balance sheet is:

(Cumulative temporary difference) * % tax rate

Marginal tax rate (MTR)

This is the tax rate that should be applied to the next unit of profit. It is normally equivalent to the corporate tax rate in the relevant country.

Effective rax rate (ETR)

The *effective tax rate* is the average tax rate applied to the profit before tax. It is calculated as:

Tax rate?

Make sure you are using the correct one!

$$\frac{\textbf{Tax expense}}{\textbf{Profit before tax}} = \textbf{Effective tax rate \%}$$

So why might this rate be different to the marginal tax rate described above. Well, there may be some expenses in the income statement / profit and loss account which are not recognized as *"deductible"* by the tax authorities. In this case the *taxable profit* will be bigger than profit before tax. There may also be some items of income in the income statement / profit and loss account which are not *"taxable"* which will cause taxable profit to be smaller than profit before tax in the income statement / profit and loss account. These are the *permanent differences* described above and their existence causes differences between MTR and ETR.

It is important to note that *differences between ETR and MTR are never due to temporary differences* since these are adjusted for in the balance sheet. The tax expense is an accrued number and therefore does not pay any attention to the period in which the cash flow is expected to take place. Therefore deferred taxes are embedded in the tax expense calculation in the same way as cash taxes are.

It is the existence of permanent differences that causes the ETR to diverge from the MTR.

Avis Cooper Ltd - part 1:

Avis Cooper Ltd reported profits before tax of 260. The depreciation expense in the income statement / profit and loss account was 50 but the depreciation deductible for taxes was 110. The tax rate was 30%.

In this case the tax expense reported in the income statement / profit and loss account is 78 (260 * 30%). This tax expense can be split into current and deferred elements as follows:

- Current taxes 60 ((260 + 50 - 110) * 30%) and
- Deferred taxes of 18 ((110 - 50) * 30%)

This split is shown on the balance sheet, but not in the income statement, although the footnotes often provide the tax expense split shown above.

It is important to note that in this case ETR (78 / 260) is 30% just like the MTR. This is because there is only a temporary difference which does not affect the ETR.

Avis Cooper Ltd - part 2:

Using the same information as in part 1 we now understand that there are expenses in SG&A of 30 which are not deductible for taxes.

In this case the tax expense reported in the income statement / profit and loss account is 87 ((260 + 30) * 30%). This tax expense can be split into current and deferred elements as follows:

ETR ≠ MTR?

This is due to permanent differences NOT timing differences

- Current taxes 69 ((260 + 30 + 50 - 110) * 30%) and
- Deferred taxes of 18 ((110 - 50) * 30%)

It is important to note that in this case ETR (87 / 260) is 33% whereas the MTR is only 30%. This is because there is an adverse permanent difference which causes the average taxes to be 3% higher than the marginal tax rate.

So, in summary, differences between ETR and MTR are only caused by permanent differences.

Deferred taxes assets and liabilities

Like a prepaid expense or an accrued expense

Although some accountants may blanche at the analogy, you can think of deferred tax assets like **prepaid tax expenses** and deferred tax liabilities like **accrued tax expenses**. The best way to explain deferred taxes is to look at an example:

Strongman Steel Inc.

Strongman Steel Inc. is a mid-Western steel business producing heavy metal products for the construction industry. Linda Zeppelin, the CEO, was looking at a five-year projection for the business (assume all figures are in millions):

	Year 1	Year 2	Year 3	Year 4	Year 5
Sales	1,000	1,300	1,500	1,600	1,650
Expenses	(850)	(1,050)	(1,250)	(1,400)	(1,420)
Profit	150	250	250	200	230

Linda was deciding whether to invest in a specialist steel press known in the business as the "Thin Lizzy". One Thin Lizzy costs $300m and lasts approximately five years. Linda estimates the Thin Lizzy will have minimal salvage value at the end of its life.

Thin Lizzy's depreciation

Strongman Steel's accountant, Jim Propeller-Head, gave Linda two depreciation profiles, one for tax and one for GAAP:

Thin Lizzy depreciation schedule

	TAX	GAAP
Year 1	150	60
Year 2	100	60
Year 3	50	60
Year 4	0	60
Year 5	0	60

Strongman Steel's income statement

Linda revised her projections and prepared two income statements:

Strongman Steel's GAAP income statement

	Year 1	Year 2	Year 3	Year 4	Year 5
Sales	1,000	1,300	1,500	1,600	1,650
Expenses	(850)	(1,050)	(1,250)	(1,400)	(1,420)
Thin Lizzy Depr.	(60)	(60)	(60)	(60)	(60)
Profit before tax	90	190	190	140	170
Tax exp @ 30%	(27)	(57)	(57)	(42)	(51)

She then looked at the impact on Strongman's tax accounts:

Strongman Steel's TAX income statement

	Year 1	Year 2	Year 3	Year 4	Year 5
Sales	1,000	1,300	1,500	1,600	1,650
Expenses	(850)	(1,050)	(1,250)	(1,400)	(1,420)
Thin Lizzy Depr.	(150)	(100)	(50)	0	0
Profit before tax	0	150	200	200	230
Tax exp @ 30%	0	(45)	(60)	(60)	(69)

Cash crossover

Although a company's tax and GAAP accounts are separate, cash on the GAAP balance sheet is the crossover account. You can't record cash changes differently. Taxes due affect cash while tax expense does not!

How do you get the balance sheet to balance? For example, in Year 1 retained earnings falls by 27 because of tax expense for the year but no cash taxes are paid so cash stays the same.

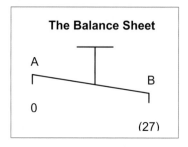

The Balance Sheet

A

B

0

(27)

Deferred taxes to the rescue!

Although tax expense in the early years is higher than taxes paid the situation reverses in later years:

	Year 1	Year 2	Year 3	Year 4	Year 5
Tax expense	(27)	(57)	(57)	(42)	(51)
Tax due	0	(45)	(60)	(60)	(69)

The total tax expense and tax due is the same (both total 234). Only the TIMING of the tax expense and due is different. Deferred taxes help us to balance the balance sheet:

Changes to the asset side of the balance sheet

	Year 1	Year 2	Year 3	Year 4	Year 5
Tax due	0	(45)	(60)	(60)	(69)

Changes to the liability and equity side of the balance sheet

	Year 1	Year 2	Year 3	Year 4	Year 5
Tax expense	(27)	(57)	(57)	(42)	(51)
Δ Def. Tax liability	27	12	(3)	(18)	(18)

As you can see, the deferred tax liability grows and then declines in "old age".

Balance

Def. Tax liability	27	39	36	18	0

Is that it?!

Sadly not. There are **two** types of deferred taxes. **Deferred tax liabilities** which you have just been introduced to and **deferred tax assets**.

Deferred tax assets are created when you start paying tax before you start expensing it.

Unwind

Deferred taxes have a shelf life. They unwind and don't keep going forever. If a company's deferred tax accounts continue to grow, they are being replenished faster than they are unwinding

A good example is a restructuring reserve:

Diskco and Steve Stiffsquare

Diskco is the leading manufacturer of floppy disks in North America. Steve Stiffsquare, Diskco's CEO, refused to believe the internet would amount to anything and stuck to solely making floppy disks. Steve maintained his strategy despite warnings from several shareholders that the floppy disk would be a thing of the past in five years. Three years later, Steve was awarded early retirement by the unanimous vote of the board.

Jack Newblood was hired as CEO to turn around Diskco. Jack estimated it would cost over $300m, spread over 3 years, to turn Diskco around. How do you account for the restructuring charges?

- Under US GAAP, restructuring charges are expensed as soon as they can be estimated
- Under US tax accounting, restructuring costs are only deductible when they are paid in cash

Jack Newblood's GAAP income statement forecast

	Year 1	Year 2	Year 3
Sales	1,200	1,200	1,400
Expenses	(600)	(800)	(900)
Restructuring costs	(300)	0	0
Profit before tax	300	400	500
Tax @ 30%	(90)	(120)	(150)

Jack Newblood's TAX income statement forecast

	Year 1	Year 2	Year 3
Sales	1,200	1,200	1,400
Expenses	(600)	(800)	(900)
Restructuring costs	(100)	(100)	(100)
Profit before tax	500	300	400
Tax @ 30%	(150)	(90)	(120)

Jack Newblood's GAAP balance sheet forecast

	Year 1	Year 2	Year 3
Assets			
Δ Cash	(150)	(90)	(120)
Δ Deferred tax asset	60	(30)	(30)
L&E			
Δ Retained earnings	(90)	(120)	(150)

As you can see, the deferred tax asset grows and then declines in "old age".

Def tax asset	60	30	0

Warning! Don't mix up your assets and liabilities

Deferred tax assets and liabilities relate to individual transactions. When a deferred tax liability starts to unwind, DON'T start recording a deferred tax asset!

Deferred taxes - what creates them

Lots of different situations create deferred tax assets and liabilities. Some of the more common ones are listed below:

Deferred tax assets	Deferred tax liabilities
■ Coupon expense ■ Restructuring reserve ■ OPEBS ■ Warranty expense ■ NOLs	■ Payroll taxes ■ Accelerated depreciation ■ Deductible goodwill ■ Revaluation of PP&E in an acquisition

Tax losses

Loss relief

When a company makes losses the government helps out by letting the company carry back the losses for offset against taxes paid in previous years. In this case you are asking for a repayment of prior year's taxes paid. Alternatively, you can carry forward the losses for offset against taxable income in future years. In this case, in some future year, you will not have any taxes to pay even though you made profits. The rules vary from country to country but for example in the US:

■ You can CARRY BACK losses for two years
■ You can CARRY FORWARD losses twenty years
■ For operating losses made before August 6, 1997 you can carry forward 15 years and carry back 3 years

Losses!

Can you get some tax benefit?

Loss carry backs

Before we take a look at an example some KEY POINTS:

■ Loss carry backs are set off against the prior year's profits
■ The loss carry backs help reduce the losses on the income statement / profit and loss account by adding a tax refund
■ Use the historical tax rate to calculate the tax loss carry back
■ Start applying the loss to the earliest year you can carry back

Confused? OK, here is an example to shed some light on tax loss carry backs.

Eleanor Rigby

Eleanor Rigby ran a fast growing dating agency "For all you lonely people" Inc ("FAYLP"). Over the last twelve months Eleanor had hired fifteen new dating consultants. It takes at least six months for Eleanor to train the consultants before they are revenue generating. The expansion increased expenses so much that FAYLP Inc. recorded a loss of $200k for the year.

FAYLP Inc. accounts.

Figures in 000s	Hist - 3	Hist - 2	Hist - 1	Current year
Sales	500	800	1,000	1,100
Expenses	(400)	(700)	(750)	(1,300)
Operating Profit (loss)	100	100	250	(200)
Effective tax rate	30%	32%	30%	
Tax expense	(30)	(32)	(75)	62
Profit after tax	70	68	175	(138)

Calculating FAYLP Inc's tax loss carry back.

Losses in the current year = (200)

Hist - 2	100 * 32%	=	32
Hist - 1	100 * 30%	=	30
Total carry back		=	**62**

Loss carry forwards

Loss carry forwards work in a similar way to loss carry backs except (of course!) you carry forward the losses to future years. However, there is a snag. And since we are referring to tax returns not yet filed with the tax authorities then any tax asset created is a deferred tax asset. In most countries you can only offset losses against profits from a similar trade or business. Therefore we have a potential tax asset which will only be realized if a loss-making business turns around to become profitable.

Consequently, most countries rules suggest that you do not recognize this type of deferred tax asset unless it is probable that it will crystallize. Any such asset is measured using the estimated future tax rate.

Let's take a look at an example before going any further.

Sergeant Pepper!

Sergeant Pepper Ltd. prepares luxury lunches for leading Investment Banks on Wall Street. Sergeant Pepper is in a highly seasonal business and usually makes losses in the bottom of the economic cycle. Iva Nosleep, an analyst at an investment bank, is asked to prepare a forecast of Sergeant Pepper for the next five years. Assume Sergeant Pepper cannot carry back any tax losses. Iva's forecast is below:

Year	PBT	Tax Rate	Tax	Def Tax Asset	Cash Taxes
Current year	(200)	30%	n / a	60	0
Project 1	50	30%	15	45	0
Project 2	100	30%	30	15	0
Project 3	150	30%	45	0	30
Project 4	200	30%	60	0	60

In the current year Sergeant Pepper makes $(200) of losses before tax. As Sergeant Pepper is a cyclical company Iva expects to be able to offset the losses in future years. She then creates a loss carry forward benefit on the income statement / profit and loss account to the tune of $60 = 200 * 30%, and a $60 deferred tax asset.

Assets	=	Liabilities and Equity
Deferred tax asset ↑		Equity ↑
		(retained earnings goes up as tax expense goes down)

Over the next four years Iva forecasts the deferred tax asset being used up, helping to conserve cash flow. Tax payments get back to normal by the fourth projected year.

Taxes and deals

There are two issues to be dealt with in a deal situation:

- The impact of goodwill and
- The impact of any asset step-ups

Goodwill and taxes

When a business is interested in buying another business it can gain control by buying the equity (an equity deal) or by buying all the individual assets and liabilities instead (an asset deal). The latter might be more attractive, for example, if you specifically wanted to exclude some of the liabilities of the target.

There is no difference in the consolidated numbers reported between an asset or equity deal. The purpose of consolidated accounts is to show the underlying economics of the situation and to bypass the legal details. This also has no impact on taxes because most of the time the consolidated numbers are ignored for the purposes of calculating tax liabilities. What is important for calculating taxes is the financials of the legal entity which bought the equity or the assets.

An equity deal

If the parent buys the equity of another then, in the *parent balance sheet*, this is simply reported as a financial investment at cost. The cost is not broken down into the component parts (assets, liabilities and goodwill) as happens in the consolidated balance sheet. As a direct consequence of this no goodwill is recognized and therefore no goodwill amortization is tax deductible. (Remember, the tax deduction rules don't necessarily bear any relationship with the accounting rules so the fact that there is no accounting amortization of goodwill is largely irrelevant). This means that, although in most countries goodwill amortization is tax deductible, in fact, it is not deductible on equity deals simply because no goodwill is recognized in the parent's standalone balance sheet.

An asset deal

If the parent buys the net assets of another then, in the **parent balance sheet**, this is reported by recording all the detailed assets and liabilities purchased. Since it is likely that a premium above book was paid then this too must be recorded in order for the balance sheet to balance. This means that the goodwill is being recorded in the parent's balance sheet directly and since this is the primary reporting entity for taxes it also stands that this goodwill may qualify for tax amortization. Needless to say this is potentially very valuable for the buyer so it begs the question: Why are deals not always done like this? Actually, generally speaking, asset deals are tax advantageous for the buyer (for the reasons outlined) but are tax disadvantageous to the seller. In other words, buyers often like asset deals but sellers often do not.

Summary

It is also worth noting that the value of goodwill calculated for tax purposes may be different to that calculated for accounting purposes as tax rules differ to accounting rules.

In the consolidated financials (which we are concerned with):

1. For equity deals:

   Goodwill is not usually amortized for GAAP or taxes purposes. Therefore there is no difference between GAAP and taxes, and consequently it can be ignored when calculating tax expense, taxes payable and deferred tax balances.

2. For asset deals:

   Goodwill is not amortized for GAAP but may be amortized for taxes. This means that there is a difference between GAAP amortization (zero) and tax amortization (often amortized over 15 years). This is considered to be a timing difference since the GAAP goodwill may be expensed in the income statement if an impairment is recognized in the future or on the eventual sale of the business. Depending on the GAAP, a deferred tax asset or liability may need to be recognized on the difference between GAAP goodwill and tax goodwill. The tax rules in this area are complex and the advice of a specialist should be sought if needed.

Asset step-ups and taxes

A similar problem arises as a result of an issue associated with goodwill. It is to do with the stepping up of assets when you do a fair value adjustment in order to calculate goodwill. Again, the tax authorities are primarily concerned with the legal entity rather than the consolidated financials so the question arises about whether these step-ups arise in the target financials (and are potentially recognizable for taxes) or whether they arise only in the consolidated numbers. Once again, the main driver of the matter is the legal structure of the deal, are we buying the equity of the target or are we buying the assets / liabilities of the target.

Goodwill!

Equity deal

No issue - ignore

Asset deal

Adjust for tax-deductible goodwill amortization. DT may be relevant

The key issue here is if we are stepping up the assets then the basis for calculating depreciation has increased and so will depreciation. So the question becomes one of whether the new asset basis is recognized for tax purposes. This is important because an increased tax depreciation schedule is clearly valuable to the buyer.

An equity deal

Here we are buying the target's equity from the target's shareholders. From a legal viewpoint (and hence tax viewpoint) the assets have not been bought by anyone (before the deal they were owned by the target and after the deal they are still owned by the target) so therefore there is no change in basis.

Asset step-ups!

Equity deal
Include the DT impact of any assets step-ups

Asset deal
No issue - ignore

An asset deal

Here the assets have legally changed hands. Pre-deal they were owned by the target and post-deal they are owned by the buyer. The question is what amount the buyer paid for this particular asset. To figure this out the purchase price (for the whole business) must be divided into its component parts and this gives the value of the assets at their stepped up amount. From a tax perspective, the owner has changed so there is a new tax basis; the stepped up value, which means that higher tax depreciation will accrue.

Summary

In the consolidated financials (which we are concerned with):

1. For equity deals:

    The assets are stepped up for GAAP and increased depreciation expense arises. The assets are not stepped up for taxes so no extra tax depreciation arises. This causes an **EXTRA difference between GAAP and taxes which must be reflected by EXTRA deferred tax**. The extra deferred tax is calculated as follows:

    Step-up * % tax rate

    So, in an equity deal situation, if you step up the assets as part of the goodwill calculation, you must also include the deferred tax impact of the step-up.

2. For asset deals:

    The assets are stepped up for GAAP and increased depreciation expense arises. The assets are also stepped up for taxes and therefore extra tax depreciation arises too. This means that the difference between GAAP and taxes is the same as it was pre-deal. Consequently there are no implications on the reported tax numbers and the step-ups can be ignored when calculating tax expense, taxes payable and deferred taxes.

    So, in an asset deal situation, if you step up the assets as part of the goodwill calculation, you should not include any deferred tax impact since none actually exists.

Earnings per share

Two types of earnings per share

In most countries, companies show two types of earnings per share in their accounts:

- Basic earnings per share and
- Diluted earnings per share

Basic earnings per share

Divides income / profit to common or ordinary shareholders by the weighted average common shares outstanding during the year.

Diluted earnings per share

Shows what might happen to EPS in the future in the "worst case scenario". This recalculates the basic earnings per share assuming all potentially dilutive securities actually result in share issues.

Basic earnings per share

Take the earnings available to common or ordinary stockholders and compare it to the weighted average common shares outstanding.

Basic earnings per share

Net income less pref. dividend

Weighted average common shares outstanding

The top part

You can't simply take net income or profit after tax as the numerator in the basic earnings per share calculation. You must subtract dividends paid to preference shareholders first. The earnings per share calculations are only interested in income / profit available to *common / ordinary shareholders*.

$$\frac{\text{Net income - Preference dividends}}{\text{Weighted average shares outstanding}} = \text{Basic EPS}$$

The bottom part

The bottom of the equation takes the weighted average shares outstanding. If there were any shares issued during the year these are weighted for the proportion of the year in issue and included in the calculation. Remember, *outstanding shares* are issued shares minus shares repurchased (treasury stock).

Jennifer's Jitneys

Jennifer manages a bus service to the Hamptons during the summer months in New York. She gives you the following information:

- Projected net income for the year to 31 December is $22m. She also has to pay $3m in preference dividends
- At the beginning of the year Jennifer had 30m shares outstanding. During the year she made the following transactions:
  - She repurchased 2m shares on June 30
  - 4m shares were issued on March 31 as a result of executive share options being exercised

Watch out for!

Share changes during the year. You need to calculate the weighted average number of shares outstanding

Numerator:	$22m - $3m	=	$19m

Denominator:	30m * 12 / 12	=	30m
	(2m) * 6 / 12	=	(1m)
	4m * 9 / 12	=	3m
	Total	=	32m

Basic EPS	19m / 32m	=	$0.59

Diluted earnings per share

Basic earnings per share is the *simple* calculation. Diluted earnings per share focuses on the *worst case scenario* for investors. Investors want to know how their interest could be diluted by the existence of other securities that have the right to convert into common stock or ordinary shares. More common / ordinary shares means there will be fewer earnings to share around!

Potentially dilutive securities

Diluted EPS?

If all the contractual obligations to issue shares are met and earnings do not increase

Potentially dilutive securities are securities which *could* convert into common stock at a later date. A few examples include:

- Executive share options (not traded options)
- Convertible bonds
- Warrants
- Convertible preferred stock
- Earn outs (where new shares are issued)

Deciding whether to convert or not

The diluted earnings per share calculates what could happen if the potentially dilutive securities, *hypothetically*, were converted. The technique is known as the *"as if converted method"*. A few points first:

- Only convert securities if they will *dilute* earnings per share. Options issued by the company that are in the money will dilute earnings per share, but options not in the money will be *anti-dilutive* (they will increase earnings per share)
- Weight the potentially dilutive securities if they were issued after the beginning of the year
- If some potentially dilutive securities did convert during the year you should apply the "as if converted method" to the securities for the period before conversion

Executive share options - in the money?

The treasury method is a way of measuring the **potential dilution** to EPS as a result of outstanding executive share options being exercised.

The first step is to determine whether the options are **in the money** or not. If the option's **strike price** (the price at which the option holder can buy stock) is lower than the **average** stock price for the year then the option holders have a deal and are in the money.

The Treasury method

Jennifer's Jitneys again!

Let's go back to Jennifer's Jitneys. On June 30 Jennifer awarded 2m stock options to the CFO of Jennifer's Jitneys with a strike price of $10. At the end of the year Jennifer was working out the **diluted** earnings per share for the company. The average share price for the year was $12.

The diluted earnings per share calculation looks at the worst case scenario and since the options are **in the money** we want to look at the potential impact on earnings per share.

If the options were exercised, Jennifer would have to issue 2m new shares.

However, Jennifer would receive $10 * 2m from the option holders on exercise, a total of $20m.

We assume Jennifer uses the spare cash to **repurchase her own shares**, in order to minimize the dilutive effect.

How many shares could she repurchase? $20m / $12 equals a total of 1.7m shares repurchased.

So the situation need not be as bad as we originally thought as 2m new shares minus 1.7m shares repurchased equals 0.3m **net new shares**.

The options were only outstanding for six months of the year so we need to weight the 0.3m shares by 6 / 12 to get 0.15m shares.

The ending impact on the EPS denominator is 0.15m shares.

To recap:

Money received from option holders	$10 * 2m	= $20m
Money used to repurchase shares	$20m / $12	= 1.7m
Net new shares	2m - 1.7m	= 0.3m
Weighting	0.3m * (6 / 12)	= 0.15m

Treasury method shortcut

Treasury method shortcut!

To save time you can use the following equation to work out the amount of incremental new shares as a result of options being exercised in a diluted EPS calculation (before weighting):

$$\text{Number of options} \times \left(\frac{\text{Average share price - Exercise price}}{\text{Average market price}} \right) = \text{Net new shares}$$

Convertible bonds

We're not out of the woods yet. One of the more complicated situations you will come across is dealing with convertible bonds. Convertible bonds impact the earnings per share calculation in *TWO* ways. If the bonds convert:

- The company will have *less* interest expense
- The company will have *more* shares outstanding

The impact on the earnings to common / ordinary shareholders

Without the interest from the convertible bond the company would have less interest expense, more profit before tax, more tax expense and more income / profit to common / ordinary shareholders.

To calculate the impact on the earnings to common / ordinary shareholders *add back* the interest on the convertible bond after subtracting the interest tax shield:

Jennifer's Jitneys again!

In the following year Jennifer asked you to calculate the diluted earnings per share using the following information.

Jennifer's projected net income / profit after tax for the year is $25m. She also has to pay $3m in preference dividends.

At the beginning of the year Jennifer had 52m shares outstanding. During the year she made the following transactions:

- A convertible bond issue on January 1 for $100m with a coupon rate of 3%. The bonds were issued at a par value of $1,000. Each bond converts into 100 common shares. The effective tax rate is 30%
- A repurchase of 4m shares on June 30
- Assume no share options are outstanding

Basic earnings	$25m - $3m	= $22m
Interest saved	$100m * 3 % * (1 - 30%)	= $2.1m
Adjusted earnings		= $24.1m
Basic WASO	52m - (4m * 6 / 12)	= 50m
New shares to be issued	$100m / $1,000 * 100	= 10m
Diluted WASO		= 60m
Basic EPS	22 / 50	= $0.44
Diluted EPS	24.1 / 60	= $0.40

Watch out for anti-dilutive securities

Don't include any potentially dilutive securities if they *increase* EPS. Testing whether a security is anti-dilutive can get complicated when you have lots of different securities in your diluted EPS calculation. Here's how to approach that situation:

- First rank the securities in order of earnings per incremental share from the lowest to the highest
- Then add in each security one by one and stop when the next most dilutive security increases the earnings per share

Phoney Tunes!

Look at the following example illustrating how to deal with a company that has many potentially dilutive securities.

Phoney Tunes is a leading country music record company. John Wynette the CFO of Phoney Tunes was preparing to calculate the company's basic and diluted earnings per share. First he set out the following information for the year ended 31 December:

1. Total shares outstanding at the beginning of the year were 45m.
2. Total earnings available to common shareholders are $23m.
3. On March 31st John Wynette repurchased 5m shares.
4. At the beginning of the year the senior executive option scheme had the following options outstanding:
   - 5m options with a strike price of $11
   - 12m options with a strike price of $9
5. The company's average stock price during the year was $10.
6. In previous years Phoney Tunes had issued two convertibles:
   - $50m 4% convertible potentially converting into 5m shares
   - $20m 7% convertible potentially converting into 1m shares
7. The effective tax rate for the company was 35%.

Step 1:

First calculate the basic earnings per share:

Basic earnings		= 23m
Basic WAS	45m - 5m * 9 / 12	= 41.25m
Basic EPS	23m / 41.25m	= $0.56

Step 2:

Rank the securities in order of their dilution (most dilutive first):

Security	Income impact	Share impact	EPS per net new share
Options	0.00	1.20	$0.00
		12m * (10 - 9 / 10)	
$50m Conv.	1.30	5.00	$0.26
	$50m * 4% * (1 - 35%)		1.30 / 5.00
$20m Conv.	0.91	1.00	$0.91
	$20m * 7% * (1 - 35%)		0.91 / 1.00

Remember to exclude any options not in the money.

Step 3:

Now add in each dilutive security in order:

Security	Income to common shareholders	Common shares	Earnings per share
Basic	23.00	41.25	$0.56
Options	0.00	1.20	
Subtotal	**23.00**	**42.45**	**$0.54**
$50m bonds	1.30	5.00	
Subtotal	**24.30**	**47.45**	**$0.51**
$20m bonds	0.91	1.00	
Subtotal	**25.21**	**48.45**	**$0.52**

In this case diluted earnings per share are $0.51.

In the example above you must stop your dilutive earnings per share calculation at the second subtotal or when diluted earnings per share are $0.51. The 20m convertible bonds are anti-dilutive. If you include the 20m convertible bonds you actually increase the diluted earnings per share.

Complex debt

Discounted bonds and PIK notes

Normal debt

Normally when debt is issued the terms in the loan documentation will specify that the interest is to be paid in cash (often referred to as "cash pay") on the due date and it also specifies when the principal will be repaid. The repayments of principal can be over the length of the loan or in one lump at the end. If they are repaid over the course of the loan life (the tenor) then this is referred to as amortizing debt. If the principal is repaid in a lump sum at the end of the life then it is called a bullet repayment.

The accounting engineering for normal debt

When the loan is taken out:

Assets	=	Liabilities and Equity
Cash ↑		Debt ↑

When interest is paid in cash on the due date:

Assets	=	Liabilities and Equity
Cash ↓		Equity ↓
		(Interest expense decreases retained earnings)

And when a repayment of principal is made:

Assets	=	Liabilities and Equity
Cash ↓		Debt ↓

PIK notes

PIK means "paid in kind" and typically refers to the interest element of the commitment. Here the lender is agreeing that the interest due is not paid in cash but instead is added onto the amount of the loan. This means that over time the interest is accrued and the amount of the debt will increase by the unpaid interest.

The accounting engineering for PIK notes

When the loan is taken out:

Assets	=	Liabilities and Equity
Cash ↑		Debt ↑

When interest is accrued:

Assets	=	Liabilities and Equity
		Debt ↑
		Equity ↓
		(Interest expense decreases retained earnings)

And when a repayment is made:

Assets	=	Liabilities and Equity
Cash ↓		Debt ↓

Interest is calculated as follows:

Beginning debt amount * interest rate

Since the debt is increasing each period by the amount of the unpaid interest, so too the interest expense gets bigger each period. This reflects the compounding nature of such an arrangement. Essentially, PIK notes are issued at par and redeemed at a premium to compensate for the unpaid interest over the loan duration.

Discounted bonds

Something similar happens when bonds are issued at a deep discount. The easiest to think about are zero-coupon bonds. Here the interest paid (the coupon rate) is zero. To compensate the investor they are issued at a deep discount. In this case the bonds are issued below par but redeemed at par. Economically, this is the same as the PIK notes discussed above. To achieve your goal, you can issue at par and redeem at a premium (PIK notes) or you can issue at a discount and redeem at par (deep discounted bonds). In both cases the investor is receiving more money back at the end of the life of the loan than they provided at the beginning. This is to compensate them for any unpaid interest.

Calculating the issue price:

This is time value of money calculation. The pricing is the present value of the future cash flows discounted at the yield required by investors for an investment of a similar risk profile.

For example:

Justin Pty issued a $1,000, 3-year bond with a 2% coupon rate when the market yield for a similar risk level was 6.5%. Assume annual payments.

In this case the cash flows are:

- Interest paid - Par amount * Coupon
- Redemption value - Par amount

The issue price is the present value of those flows discounted as follows:

$1,000 * 2\% / (1 + 0.065)^1$	=	18.8
$1,000 * 2\% / (1 + 0.065)^2$	=	17.6
$(($1,000 * 2\%) + 1,000) / (1 + 0.065)^3$	=	844.4

Total   **880.8**

So a $1,000 bond is issued at $880.8 in this case.

Calculating the interest numbers:

In this case there is a difference between the accrued interest and the interest paid in cash. The accrued interest is calculated in the usual way:

Beginning debt amount * interest rate

Whereas the cash interest paid as in the bond documentation is:

Par amount * coupon rate

Since the coupon rate is so much lower than the yield (and can be zero as in the case of a zero-coupon bond) this means that some of the interest expense is cash pay and some is PIK.

The accounting engineering for discounted bonds

When the loan is taken out:

Assets	=	**Liabilities and Equity**
Cash ↑		Debt ↑
		(at issue price)

When interest is accrued:

Assets	=	**Liabilities and Equity**
Cash ↓		Debt ↑
(Cash decreases by the amount of the coupon * par)		(This is the a plug number - the amount of the unpaid interest)
		Equity ↓
		(Interest expense decreases retained earnings)

And when a repayment is made:

Assets	=	**Liabilities and Equity**
Cash ↓		Debt ↓
		(Redeemed at par)

Justin Pty - continued:

On issue:

	Assets	=	Liabilities and Equity
	Cash ↑ 880.8		Debt ↑ 880.8

Year 1 interest accrued:

	Assets	=	Liabilities and Equity
	Cash ↓ 20 (1,000 * 2%)		Debt ↑ 37.3 (57.3 - 20)
			Equity ↓ 57.3 (880.8 * 6.5%)

Year 2 interest accrued:

	Assets	=	Liabilities and Equity
	Cash ↓ 20 (1,000 * 2%)		Debt ↑ 39.7 (59.7 - 20)
			Equity ↓ 59.7 ((880.8 + 37.3) * 6.5%)

Year 3 interest accrued:

	Assets	=	Liabilities and Equity
	Cash ↓ 20 (1,000 * 2%)		Debt ↑ 42.3 (62.3 - 20)
			Equity ↓ 62.3 ((880.8 + 37.3 + 39.7) * 6.5%)

And when a repayment is made:

	Assets	=	Liabilities and Equity
	Cash ↓ 1,000		Debt ↓ 1,000 (880.8 + 37.3 + 39.7 + 42.3)

Convertible debt

This is debt that has been issued with warrants (options) attached.

Under IFRS, "split accounting" is used. In this case the issue proceeds are split into the debt and equity components. The debt is shown as debt and the equity is part of shareholders' equity. This split is done at issue by checking the market value of a vanilla debt instrument (one without the warrant attached) with a similar risk profile. The difference between the implied issue price of a vanilla debt instrument and that of the convertible gives the implied valuation of the options.

Under US GAAP, convertible debt which can be cash settled (in part or in full) follows the same treatment as IFRS, however, all other convertible debt follows a very different treatment. The debt is shown as a liability with no equity element recognized until conversion actually takes place. If conversion takes place then the debt is reduced but instead of a cash decrease, shareholders' equity increases.

Leases

**Leases!
What are they all
about?**

Is it an operating or
a finance / capital
lease?

Leases are one of the most complex areas of accounting. The rules seek to identify the economic substance behind the lease. It tries to identify a lease which really is like buying an asset with a financing plan compared with a lease which is simply an asset hire agreement. These two lease types are called:

■ Finance or capital leases and
■ Operating leases

So the key questions…

Is this lease really just a way of financing the asset purchase? You can think of the difference being either buying the asset or just renting it.

Buying or renting: the rules

The tests for identifying a capital or finance lease include:

1. Ownership passes to you at the end of the lease.
2. You have a bargain purchase option.
3. The lease represents most of the asset's useful life.
4. The PV of the lease payments are ≥ 90% of the asset's fair market value at the start of the lease (per US GAAP, not under IFRS).

If these tests do not apply then the lease is an *operating lease*. Otherwise you must account for it as a *capitalized / finance lease*.

Operating leases

Operating leases are simple. Record the lease on the income statement / profit and loss as a rent expense:

Assets	=	Liabilities and Equity
Cash ↓		Equity ↓ (rent expense decreases retained earnings)

The expense matches the cash outflow. That's pretty much it.

Capitalized leases

Capitalized leases are more complicated. You account for these as though you had borrowed money to buy the asset. You need to show on the balance sheet:

■ An asset
■ A lease liability

How do you measure the liability

The capitalized lease liability is the **present value** of the future lease payments (or, under IFRS, FV of asset if lower). To calculate the present value, use the lower of:

- The lessee's incremental borrowing rate
- The implicit rate of return on the lease to the lessor

Joe Slow!

Joe Slow leased a tractor for three years. He has to account for the lease as a capitalized lease. The annual lease payment is $10m for 3 years. The relevant interest rate for calculating the present value is 9%.

$10m / (1 + 0.09)^1   = $9.2m
$10m / (1 + 0.09)^2   = $8.4m
$10m / (1 + 0.09)^3   = $7.7m
Total   **$25.3m**

The total present value is $25.3m, the amount of the *starting* lease liability on the balance sheet.

Each year the liability is "paid down" by the lease cash payment less an interest charge (calculated using the interest rate in your PV formula).

To calculate the interest, multiply the beginning balance by the interest rate. In year 1 the interest is $2.3m (25.3 * 9%). You can use a BASE analysis to help with the numbers as follows:

Use a BASE analysis for the lease liability!

	Year 1	Year 2	Year 3
Beginning balance	25.3m	17.6m	9.2m
Add - interest for the period	2.3m	1.6m	0.8m
Subtract - payments made	(10.0m)	(10.0m)	(10.0m)
Ending balance	17.6m	9.2m	0.0m

To get the reduction in the liability subtract the interest from the cash payment. *Only the interest, not the cash payment, is recorded in the income statement.*

What about the asset side?

You also have to put an asset on the balance sheet *matching* the lease liability. The asset is then *depreciated* over the shorter of the asset life or lease period. Assuming no salvage value the depreciation expense each year is $8.4m. ($25.3m / 3 years). The depreciation is shown in the income statement / profit and loss account.

And the accounting engineering!

To include the leased asset initially:

Assets	=	Liabilities and Equity
Fixed assets ↑		Lease liability ↑
$25.3m		$25.3m

To deal with the interest for the period:

| Assets | = | Liabilities and Equity |

Lease liability ↑ 2.3m

Equity ↓ 2.3m
(Interest expense
decreases retained
earnings)

To deal with cash payments for the period:

| Assets | = | Liabilities and Equity |

Cash ↓   Lease liability ↓
$10.0m $10.0m

Summary

	Operating lease	Capitalized lease
Income statement	Rent expense	Interest
		Depreciation
Balance sheet		Asset
		Lease liability

Over the life of the lease the total amount of expense hitting the income statement is the same for both the operating and capitalized lease. Only the timing is different.

	Operating lease	Capital / finance lease		
	Rent expense	Interest	Depreciation	Total
Year 1	$10.0	$2.3	$8.4	$10.7
Year 2	$10.0	$1.6	$8.4	$10.0
Year 3	$10.0	$0.8	$8.4	$9.3
Total	$30.0			$30.0

Making apples into oranges

A common difficulty generated by lease accounting is comparing two companies' enterprise value where one has operating leases and the other has capitalized leases. Capital / finance leases are included in the net debt in an enterprise value calculation, but there is no debt number with an operating lease. Because the accounting is **rules based** the economic difference between the two leases may be very small, so if leasing is significant in the sector you will need to make an adjustment so that you are comparing like with like. The common adjustment is to convert the operating leases into capitalized leases one of two possible valuation methodologies

- ◾ A multiple method or
- ◾ A discounted cash based approach

As is always the case with valuation, these are estimates of what the equivalent "debt" number would be had the lease in question been structured as a capital / finance lease instead of an operating one. There is no "right" answer to this process.

Multiple method

Debt equivalent

Multiple method

Calculate the equivalent liability for an operating lease…

Rental expense * factor
(most commonly 8)

The multiple method takes the most recent operating lease expense and multiplies by a factor to convert it into the equivalent lease liability of a capitalized lease. An eight times multiple is pretty widely used for this purpose but there are many variations, five and seven being the most common variants.

Tweedle Dum and Tweedle Dee!

Tweedle Dum Inc. and Tweedle Dee Ltd. both operate transatlantic airfreight services. Tweedle Dum Inc. capitalizes leases while Tweedle Dee Ltd accounts for leases using the operating method. The following table shows an EBITDA multiples analysis of the two companies.

	Tweedle Dum	Tweedle Dee
Operating lease expense	0.0	10.0
Rule of 8 lease liability	0.0	80.0
Lease liability	100.0	0.0
Debt	300.0	400.0
Cash	50.0	40.0
Net debt	**350.0**	**440.0**
Market cap.	600.0	800.0
Enterprise value	**950.0**	**1,240.0**
EBITDA	170.0	230.0
EBITDA + op. lease expense	170.0	240.0
EBITDA Enterprise multiple	**5.6x**	**5.2x**

Calculations for Tweedle Dee

Rule of 8 lease liability	=	Operating lease exp. * 8
	=	10 * 8 = 80
Net debt	=	leases + debt - cash
	=	80 + 400 - 40
Enterprise value	=	net debt + market cap.
	=	440 + 800
EBITDA + operating lease expense	=	230 + 10
EBITDA enterprise multiple	=	1,240 / 240

EBITDA adjustment

Remember to **add** the operating lease expense back to EBITDA so you are not including any expenses related to the leasing of assets in your multiple. Capitalized leases are expensed via depreciation and interest and EBITDA excludes both these expenses.

NI and EBIT adjustments

If you want to use NI or EBIT multiples you should make the necessary adjustments for depreciation and interest to the earnings when you are "capitalizing" operating leases. Making these adjustments turns out to be difficult given the sketchy information contained in a published financials. If leases are important to the businesses of both companies then most analysts will stick with EBITDA multiples.

AdkinsMatchett&Toy

Complex debt

DCF method

Debt equivalent

In order to apply a DCF approach you need the following information:

- Forecast cash flows
- Timing of those cash flows
- Appropriate discount rate

In the published financials, it is common to be given the forecast operating lease rentals for the following 5 years. However, the first problem we come across is the cash flows post year five. These are given in one single number so an estimate will have to be made about the timing of those cash flows. A common approach is to take the year 5 cash flow and assume it stays steady until you reach the total amount disclosed post year 5.

Regarding the discount rate, there are many possible choices but it is common to use the incremental cost of debt.

The most important analytic point to note regarding this method is that if you use the disclosed future cash flows, then what you are given is actually not the forecast operating lease cash flows but the *minimum contractual future cash flows*. This can sometimes be significantly smaller than the expected lease rental (compare the first future year with the lease rental for the most recent historical year to get a view). In this case, you may feel that the liability is understated. It may be worth using an estimated cash flow forecast build by looking at the past operating lease cost trend.

EBITDA adjustment

This is the same as for the multiple method.

NI and EBIT adjustments

Again, these are the same as for the multiple method.

Pensions

Introduction

Pensions are often part of the agreed compensation for services rendered. Normal remuneration is paid relatively quickly after the employee does the work but in the case of pensions this is not so. This is paid at a much later date compared to when the employee actually earned it.

There are two main types of plan:

■ Defined contribution or money purchase plan
■ Defined benefit or final salary plan

How plans are funded!

In the US and the UK (and other countries also) the sponsoring employer is required to set up a separate pension plan vehicle where both the plan assets and the liability to pay pensioners legally sit. This is normally in a trust fund. This system means that the plan assets are distinguished and ring fenced from the general assets of the business. In theory, if the employer goes bankrupt then the pension assets are safe. The accounting implication is that both the fund assets and liabilities are "off balance sheet".

In some other countries (Germany, France and Japan for example) the pension is not distinguished from the corporation. The pension will be paid, not from a separate pool of assets, but from the general assets of the employer. Both the assets and the liability to pay pensions are part of the assets and liabilities of the business and sit on the balance sheet of the sponsor / employer. In these countries there is normally some form of required insurance provision which covers the pension plan in the case of bankruptcy. Also, in countries where these plans are the norm, generally most of an individual's pension will come from the state in any event.

Defined contribution (money purchase) plans

What are they?

Defined contribution plans

The *most common* plan nowadays

Investment risk is borne by the employee

They are those where the employment contract specifies that a certain amount will be set aside for the eventual pension. The level of contribution is often defined as a % of current salary. These contributions may be made by the employer, employee or a combination of both. The important criterion is that no guarantee is made about the eventual level of pension payment. If the plan does well then the pension may be a good one, however the reverse is also true. A 401K plan in the US is an example of a defined contribution plan.

Remember, in this case the contribution is fixed but the pension is variable.

How the accounting works!

This is the easy one. The accounting follows the timing of when the employee earned the contribution made on their behalf and since this is defined in the plan rules it is simple to calculate and deal with. If the plan is funded, a cash payment is made to the fund and operating expenses are increased by that amount. If the plan is unfunded then a provision is made for the pension earned with a corresponding expense included in operating costs.

For a funded plan:

Assets	=	Liabilities and Equity
Cash ↓		Equity ↓
		(Operating expenses increase)

For an unfunded plan:

Assets	=	Liabilities and Equity
		Pension provision ↑
		Equity ↓
		(Operating expenses increase)

Defined benefit (final salary) plans

What are they?

These are those plans where the employment contract specifies that a certain level of pension will be paid eventually. In this case, the employer is guaranteeing that the employee will enjoy a specified pension level in retirement. The level is often defined as a % of the average salary earned during the last five years of employment. This poses a problem for the employer. How much do they pay into the plan now in order to meet the eventual obligation to pay this level of pension? This is where the *actuary* comes in.

Remember, in this case the pension is fixed but the contribution is variable.

What the actuary does!

The actuary examines the plan rules, and makes a series of assumptions about things such as:

- Retirement age
- Mortality rates
- Number of members who are married
- Number of leavers and joiners
- Return on assets
- Salary growth rates

From all of this they estimate the expected pension obligation and how much the contribution payment should be in order that this commitment is met at the relevant date in the future.

Defined benefit plans

The numbers are all based on estimates

However!

All of this is based on estimates which may turn out to be inappropriate, so most of these plans will perform an actuarial assessment on a regular basis to check the level of funding.

The level of funding

Is based upon the following:

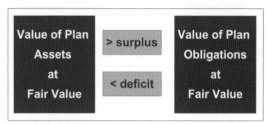

The *fair value* of the plan *assets* is normally *current market value*.

And the *fair value* of the plan *obligations* is the *present value of the estimated pension liability*. As you can imagine this value is very sensitive to the estimates mentioned above and also to the discount rate used. Normally, the discount rate used is that for a high quality corporate bond of equivalent maturity and currency.

Apart from these judgemental and complex issues there is a further issue which has a radical impact on the valuation of this obligation. That is whether you value the pension actually earned to date and base it on *current salaries* or whether you value the potential obligation and base your calculations on *projected salary*. In most accounting regimes the latter is required.

Current salary	Accumulated benefit obligation	ABO
Projected salary	Projected benefit obligation Or	PBO
	Defined benefit obligation	DBO

The PBO calculation!

PBO calculation!

Beginning PBO balance
+ Service cost The pension accrued by the employees as a result of an extra year of service to the business.
+ Interest cost The interest charged by virtue of not paying the employees for a number of years. Or, since this liability is at present value this represents the "unwinding" of one year of discount.
- Benefits paid to pensioners This represents the fact that some of the obligation has been met by paying the retired employees their pensions.
+ Prior service cost Any plan changes, usually caused by improved provisions granted to plan members for services performed in prior years.
+ / - Actuarial gains / losses Due to changes in estimates or due to reality being different to the estimate used.
Ending PBO balance

The plan assets calculation!

Plan asset calculation!

Beginning plan asset balance
+ Return on assets The return *actually* earned on the investment of the plan assets over the period.
+ Contributions The cash received by the fund from the employer (and the employee if they too contribute).
- Benefits paid to pensioners The cash paid out to pensioners.
Ending plan asset balance

So how does accounting for all this work?

In principle: the difference between plan assets and liabilities (PBO) goes on the balance sheet as an asset or a liability as appropriate.

But: the secret is to understand how it works year on year. Firstly, we are going to go through what happens assuming the estimates are all OK and there are no problem items (plan provision improvements or actuarial changes to the estimates). We will deal with these complexities when we go through the fundamentals.

The fundamentals of pension accounting

Clematis!

Clematis has a pension liability of 750,000 in its balance sheet at the beginning of the year made up as follows:

Plan assets	2,000,000
PBO	2,750,000
Under funded / Deficit	750,000

During the year the actual return on plan assets was as expected, at 130,000. Contributions were received from Clematis of 240,000 and pensions of 120,000 were paid out. The plan members earned a further 220,000 for their service and the interest cost was 165,000.

Beginning plan assets balance	2,000,000
+ Return on plan assets	130,000
+ Contributions received	240,000
- Pensions paid	120,000
Ending plan assets balance	2,250,000

Beginning PBO balance	2,750,000
+ New pensions accrued	220,000
+ Interest charged	165,000
- Pensions paid	120,000
Ending PBO balance	3,015,000

So now, at the end of the year the situation is as follows:

Plan assets	2,250,000
PBO	3,015,000
Under funded / Deficit	765,000

So the pension liability in the balance sheet of Clematis must increase by 15,000. But how does the balance sheet balance? Well, remember that cash has decreased by 240,000 because of contributions made to the fund. Operating costs are charged with the difference of 255,000, representing the pension cost for the period.

Assets	=	**Liabilities and Equity**
Cash ↓ 240,000		Net pension liability ↑ 15,000
		Equity ↓ 255,000 (Operating expenses increase)

The operating cost can be analyzed as follows:

New pensions accrued	220,000
+ Interest cost	165,000
- Return on assets	130,000
= Net pension expense	**255,000**

It is important to note that the pension cost is not the same as the pension cash flow. You should also note that the effect on earnings can be dramatically affected by the return on assets. In the 1990's many companies increased (rather than decreased) earnings because the return on assets was greater than the other components of the total pension cost.

So the fundamental principle is that the balance sheet shows the fund deficit or surplus and the expense reflects the costs of providing the plan less the return on assets set aside to meet the obligation.

The problem with return on assets and actuarial gains / losses

In the example above Clematis is artificially simple for two reasons:

- The actual return on plan assets was equal to the expected return
- There were no actuarial gains and losses

Both of these issues are very volatile and the reported numbers are highly sensitive to this volatility.

The rules allow "partial recognition" of these items. For the return on assets this is achieved by a methodology which allows inclusion of the expected rather than actual return in the income statement / profit and loss account. For the actuarial gains and losses, it is achieved via the notorious "smoothing" rules, where only a small proportion of the problem item is included in the accounting numbers. Let's look at another example:

Vitus Pty

Vitus has a pension liability of 550,000 in its balance sheet at the beginning of the year made up as follows:

Plan assets	750,000
PBO	1,300,000
Under funded / Deficit	550,000

During the year the actual return on plan assets was 52,000 while the expected return was 45,000. Contributions were received from Vitus of 140,000 and pensions of 90,000 were paid out. The plan members earned a further 120,000 due to service and the interest cost was 84,500. Furthermore, the actuary has said that an actuarial loss of 66,000 has occurred.

First, let's do the plan assets and plan obligation calculations;

Beginning plan assets balance	750,000
+ *Actual* return on plan assets	52,000
+ Contributions received	140,000
- Pensions paid	90,000
Ending plan assets balance	852,000

Beginning PBO balance	1,300,000
+ New pensions accrued	120,000
+ Interest charged	84,500
- Pensions paid	90,000
+ Actuarial loss	66,000
Ending PBO balance	1,480,500

So now, at the end of the year the situation is as follows:

Plan assets	852,000
PBO	1,480,500
Under funded / Deficit	628,500

Pensions in the balance sheet

Logically, you would expect that the balance sheet would show a liability of 628,500 *BUT*:

This is only the case when *full recognition method* is used. This is the case under US GAAP for fiscal years ending after December 15 2006. This is an option under IFRS.

Under full recognition, the balance sheet will show a liability of 628,500

BS pension asset / liability??

US GAAP
New rules - full recognition on BS

IFRS
A choice between full and partial recognition on BS

Under partial recognition, the balance sheet will show a liability as follows:

Plan assets	852,000
- PBO	1,480,500
+ / - Unamortized actuarial gains / losses - say Caused by: ■ Prior service costs ■ Actuarial gains / losses and ■ Difference between expected and actual return on plan assets (These are the amounts which "partial recognition" allows to be **OFF BALANCE SHEET**)	350,000
= Pension asset / liability	278,500

The rules for the "off balance sheet" components under the partial recognition system are detailed and complex and do not bear any relationship to the economic reality therefore from an analysts' perspective they are not very important. What is important is that an analyst can review the footnotes and see the underfunded / deficit or overfunded / surplus amounts.

Pensions in the income statement / profit and loss

Again, there are two variants, full and partial recognition (simply the effect of the choice made in the balance sheet).

Under US GAAP the partial recognition method is used while under IFRS there is currently a choice between full and partial method. The IFRS pension rules have changed and the new rules will be effective from Jan 1st 2013, with early adoption permitted. One consequence is that the partial recognition method is being abolished.

IS pension expense??

US GAAP
New rules - partial recognition in IS

IFRS
A choice between full and partial recognition in IS

Under full recognition, the income statement / profit and loss will show the following:

New pensions accrued	120,000
+ Interest cost	84,500
- **Actual** return on assets	52,000
= **Net pension expense**	**152,500**

Under this system actuarial gains / losses are recognised in full in the year they arise but they are charged directly to equity and hence have no impact on reported profits.

Under the new IFRS rules, effective from 2013, the pension expense will be made up of two components only, service cost and net interest cost on the net pension asset / liability.

Under partial recognition, the income statement / profit and loss will show the following:

New pensions accrued	120,000
+ Interest cost	84,500
- **Expected** return on assets	45,000
+ / - Part of actuarial gain / loss recognised in the current year (say)	39,000
= **Net pension expense**	**198,500**

So, in summary, the income statement / profit and loss expense is made up of:

Service cost	New pensions accrued - both methods
+ Interest cost	Increase in the PBO due to the passage of time - both methods
- Return on assets	Expected under partial method but actual under full method
+ / - Amortisation of problem items (actuarial gains / losses and prior service costs)	The amortization of the difference between actuarial assumptions and actual experience, over the expected service lives of employees - Partial method only
= **Net pension expense**	

IFRS - full recognition in the BS And IS

This is the easiest from an accounting viewpoint and works as follows:

Assets	=	Liabilities and Equity
Cash ↓ 140,000		Pension liability ↑ 78,500 (628,500 - 550,000)
		Equity ↓ 218,500 (Net expenses of 152,500 and direct to equity 66,000)

So the liability in the balance sheet goes up so that it matches the plan assets less plan obligations. The expense in the income statement / profit and loss is 152,500, made up of the service cost, interest cost less the actual return on plan assets. You should assume that these items are all treated as operating costs (in COGS or SG&A) unless the footnotes specify a different categorization.

IFRS - partial recognition in the BS and IS

In this case we need some extra information: We know that the beginning plan assets less obligations was 550,000 but under partial recognition not all of this amount will be on the balance sheet. Let us assume for this example, that 220,000 was on the balance sheet at the end of last year.

Assets	=	Liabilities and Equity
Cash ↓ 140,000		Pension liability ↑ 58,500 (278,500 - 220,000)
		Equity ↓ 198,500 (Net expenses of 198,500)

So the liability in the balance sheet is adjusted but to the level of plan assets less plan obligations less unrecognised items. The income statement / profit and loss suffers a charge of service cost, interest expense, expected return on plan assets and a portion of the problem items being recognised in the current period. Once again, you should assume that these items are all treated as operating costs (in COGS or SG&A) unless the footnotes specify a different categorization.

As noted above, the partial recognition method in the balance sheet is being abolished under IFRS from Jan 1st 2013.

US GAAP - full recognition in BS, partial recognition in IS

At the time of writing US GAAP is in flux resulting in a system which is a combination of the full and partial recognition methods. The accounting engineering is as follows:

Assets	=	Liabilities and Equity
Cash ⬇ 140,000		Pension liability ⬆ 78,500 (628,500 - 550,000)
		Equity ⬇ 218,500 (Net expenses of 198,500 and direct to equity 20,000)

The balance sheet liability goes up by the increase in the deficit. This means that the actuarial valuation numbers are being recognized in full on the balance sheet. But the income statement / profit and loss numbers continue to use the partial recognition method. Expected return on plan assets is used instead of actual return and a portion of the problem items are expenses via an amortization process. In order to get the balance sheet to balance a "plug" number is included in equity. This "plug" is actually made up of as follows:

+ Actual vs expected return on assets (52,000 - 45,000)	7,000
+ Partial recognition of problem items	39,000
- Current year actuarial loss	66,000
= Adjustment to equity required	**- 20,000**

One final point, under US GAAP the entire income statement amount is categorized as an operating item, therefore it will be embedded in either COGS or SG&A or a combination of both.

Stock awards accounting

Introduction

Stock option accounting or share based compensation accounting has changed in recent years with some associated controversy. Some hold the view that since it is not a cash cost for the business then it should not be treated as an expense like a normal salary is. Others consider that if it is not compensation then it is hard to imagine what else it could be (Warren Buffet has held this view for many years). The accounting treatment now dictates that it must be treated as an operating expense.

The fundamental logic behind the accounting

We are going to walk through an extreme example in order to highlight the issues involved. Imagine an employee gets paid $1,000 in cash for work done. This is how the accounting engineering reflects this transaction:

Assets	=	Liabilities and Equity
Cash ↓ $1,000		Equity ↓ $1,000 (Operating expenses of 1,000 reduce RE)

Now imagine that, on the same day in an entirely separate transaction, the business issues new shares for $1,000. This transaction will be reflected as follows:

Assets	=	Liabilities and Equity
Cash ↑ $1,000		Equity ↑ $1,000 (Capital increases)

As is always the case with share issues, market value changes post issue are ignored by accounting.

If the employee mentioned in the first transaction was the investor buying the shares in the second transaction, then nothing would change with regard to the accounting. This person concerned is both an employee and an investor at the same time.

So, what should we do if these two transactions are linked? Instead of paying the employee $1,000 cash for work done, we pay him or her by issuing shares worth $1,000. In fact, logically, the only thing that would change is no cash changes hands but the economic effect is the same. So when accounting for share based payments it should look like this:

Assets	=	Liabilities and Equity
		Equity ↑ $1,000 (Capital increases)
		Equity ↓ $1,000 (Operating expenses of 1,000 reduce RE)

Clearly this is a very simplistic example not least of which because it assumes shares were issued when in fact most share based compensation is in the form of options. The nature of options is that a number of additional factors need to be dealt with including:

■ The timing issue between granting, vesting and exercise and
■ The valuation issue - exactly how much is the compensation worth

Some jargon to start off

Grant date

This is when the employee is told of the detailed terms and conditions of the stock award compensation plan. The very important point about this date is that essentially the business is saying to the employee..." We will give you this number of awards if you work for a number of years and we meet the following targets".

Vesting date

This is when the employee has worked for the agreed number of years and the targets have been met. The employee is now entitled to the awards.

Exercise date

This date is when the employees "cash in" their awards. Often this can be done over an agreed time period.

Service or vesting period

This is the period during which the employee is "earning" their award entitlement by working for the business. From the above definitions, this must logically run from the date they are informed of the plan, the grant date, to the date they become entitled to them, the vesting date.

So how much compensation are we talking about?

At the grant date, the business tells a number of employees that they can earn some extra compensation (in the form of awards). At this date the business is committed provided the stock awards plan conditions are met. Consequently, we need to estimate how much we are talking about. Of course, this is easier said than done.

The stock awards should ideally be recognized at market prices but where market prices do not exist, then a valuation technique will have to be used. For stock options, the accounting rules suggest using a recognized option pricing model where possible such as:

■ Binomial or
■ Black Scholes or
■ Intrinsic value (where the first two are inappropriate)

Fundamentally, once the valuation is established **at the grant date**, then it should not be changed thereafter just as share prices are not accounted for as they change in the market. There are, however, some exceptions to this:

■ When non-market based conditions are not met
■ When the intrinsic value method is used

Non-market based conditions, such as sales growth targets, are not the same as share price changes (market based conditions) and are more like normal accounting estimates. With normal accounting estimates (like the outcome of a legal case) the fundamental principle is the numbers are adjusted in the light of new information. The same logic applies to stock options with non-market based conditions. So if some of the conditions are not met then we adjust the valuation as soon as this is known.

This does not apply to market based conditions because the probability of the conditions not being met is included as one of the inputs in the initial valuation.

Intrinsic value is considered to be a very "quick and dirty" valuation technique in this context and since it changes all the time then so should the valuation be updated each reporting period. In any event, the accounting rules intend that this is not used apart from by exception.

One final point on valuation, if the terms and conditions are modified at any stage, then the valuation must be redone. The updated numbers are used for the accounting thereafter.

How stock award expensing actually works!

So the principle is that we need to match the compensation over the time period that the employees actually work. This means that we value the awards when the employees are informed of the plan, the grant date, and then we expense that amount over the service or vesting period.

Calef Inc

Calef Inc grants an option compensation plan to employees on January 1. The vesting period is 2 years and the valuation is $300,000 when the probability of the conditions being met is ignored (non-market based) and $200,000 when the probability of conditions being met is included (market based). In year 1 the conditions are met and in year 2 they are not met. The normal attrition rate for employees leaving is 10% but by the end of the vesting period the actual attrition rate was 8%.

Market based conditions

Year 1	90,000
200,000 * 90% * 1 / 2	
(Value * no employees expected to qualify * % earned)	
Year 2	94,000
(200,000 * 92% * 2 / 2) - 90,000	
(Value * no employees entitled * % earned) less prior expense	

And the accounting engineering is as follows:

Assets = **Liabilities and Equity**

Equity ↑
(Capital increases)

Equity ↓
(Operating expenses
reduces RE)

These expenses are treated as normal operating expenses in the income statement / profit and loss. We will deal with the tax expense implications later in the chapter.

Note that there is no adjustment made for not meeting the conditions in year 2. This is because this was taken into account in the initial valuation by doing a probability weighting. It also follows the fundamental principle that the accounting does not adjust for share price changes post initial recognition.

Non market based conditions

Year 1	135,000
300,000 * 90% * 1 / 2	
(Value * no employees expected to qualify * % earned)	
Year 2	(135,000)
(0 * 92% * 2 / 2) - 135,000	
(Value * no employees entitled * % earned) less prior expense	

So the valuation in year 2 is adjusted to zero and the year 1 expenses are reversed out.

The accounting engineering in year 1 is as for market based above but in year 2 the reversal is dealt with as follows:

Assets = **Liabilities and Equity**

Equity ↓
(Capital decreases)

Equity ↑
(Operating expense
adjustment increases
RE)

Note that the valuation is adjusted in year 2 when the conditions are not met. This is because this was not taken into account in the initial valuation by omitting a probability weighting. It also follows the fundamental principle that the accounting always adjusts estimates in the light of new information.

Dealing with the tax impact in the financials

In many countries, the tax deduction is based on intrinsic value on exercise. This means that the accounting and the tax are in different time periods, accounting over vesting period and tax on exercise, and also based on different amounts, accounting on fair value and tax on intrinsic value.

There is also a difference between how these issues are dealt with under US GAAP and IFRS.

US GAAP

Under US GAAP, the recognition of deferred tax (it is deferred due to the timing nature of the difference) is based on the accounting expense. The value difference (fair value versus intrinsic value) is ignored until realized on exercise. At this stage an adjustment is made, as necessary, directly in equity.

Taking our previous example: Let's say that the options are exercised in year 3 and the intrinsic value is $170,000 at the end of year 1 and $250,000 at the end of year 2 (for those which vested). Assume a tax rate of 30%

Year	Expense	Tax expense impact	DTA
Year 1 200,000 * 90% * 1 / 2 (Value * no employees expected to qualify * % earned)	90,000	27,000	27,000
Year 2 (200,000 * 92% * 2 / 2) - 90,000 (Value * no employees entitled * % earned) less prior expense	94,000	28,200	55,200

So a deferred tax asset is recognized (future benefit to be expected in the year of exercise) based on the amounts expensed.

DTA in balance sheet at the end of year 2 (27,000 + 28,200 or (90,000 + 94,000) * 30%	55,200
Actual tax benefit earned based on intrinsic value (250,000 * 30%)	75,000
Extra benefit - directly to equity	19,800

So under US GAAP, the expense in the income statement / profit and loss and the DTA in the balance sheet are based on fair value. Intrinsic value is completely ignored until actual exercise. Any necessary adjustment to convert to intrinsic value on exercise is made directly in equity.

IFRS

IFRS is significantly different conceptually, in that intrinsic value is checked each period and:

- The DTA is based on intrinsic value
- The tax expense is based on the lower of fair value or intrinsic value (this test is done on a cumulative basis)
- Any excess of intrinsic value over fair value is taken directly to equity

Looking at the same example:

Year 1	
DTA (IV based 170,000 * 1 / 2 * 30%)	25,500
Tax expense impact (lower of FV based (27,000) and IV based (25,500)	25,500
Adjustment in equity	

Year 2	
DTA (IV based 250,000 * 2 / 2 * 30%)	75,000
Tax expense impact (lower of FV based (28,200) and IV based (75,000 - 25,500))	28,200
Adjustment in equity (49,500 (75,000 - 25,500) - 28,200)	21,300

Financial instruments

Introduction

The accounting treatment of financial instruments has evolved greatly in recent years, with an increasing focus on fair value accounting for instruments such as derivatives. Financial instruments include a wide range of items which are found in company reports:

- Cash, demand and time deposits
- Accounts receivable and payable
- Debt, loans, loan notes and commercial paper
- Equity securities
- Derivatives, including options, rights, warrants, futures contracts, forward contracts and swaps

How the financial asset or liability is accounted for will depend on its classification. There are four categories for financial assets and two for financial liabilities as shown below

Financial assets	Financial liabilities
Fair value through the income statement (FV)	Fair value through the income statement (FV)
Available-for-sale (AFS)	Other financial liabilities
Loans and receivables	
Held-to-maturity (HTM)	

Whilst this may appear complicated, there are only three different accounting techniques used:

- Fair value with changes through the income statement
- Fair value with changes recognised directly in equity
- Amortized cost accounting

The subsequent sections summarize and illustrate how each of the accounting methods work.

Fair value through the income statement (FV)

This classification is applied to both financial assets and liabilities and has two sub-headings.

Designated on initial recognition

This includes any item designated to this category on initial recognition in the accounts. This option is very unusual, and guidance suggests this should only happen where an entity actively manages the fair value of the asset or liability. You are unlikely to meet this in practice.

Held for trading

This includes all *derivatives* and instruments which are held for trading (held for the purpose of selling in the short term or where there is a recent pattern of short-term profit taking are held for trading). Financial institutions will hold instruments such as equities and bonds for trading. Almost all large corporates will hold derivatives of some kind. Commonly used derivative contracts include

- Forwards and futures
- Options
- Swaps

Items designated to this category are recognized in the balance sheet at their fair value at each reporting date (referred to as "mark-to-market"). **Any change in the fair value shown in the balance sheet is recognized in the income statement / profit and loss account for the period.**

It is unusual for accounting rules to require recognition of "unrealized" gains (if an asset increases in value, this increases income for the year despite the fact that the asset has not been sold and the gain realized). The logic behind the accounting is that derivatives and trading items are likely to be realized in the near future.

Emilan Inc

Emilan enters an interest rate swap on January 1st. The swap has a zero fair value at inception. At the December 31st year end, the swap has a positive fair value (financial asset) of $500. The accounting engineering is as follows:

Assets	=	**Liabilities and Equity**
Financial Assets ↑ $500		Equity ↑ $500 (Income statement and RE)

At the second year end the swap fair value has become negative $150. The financial asset needs to be removed and a financial liability created. The accounting engineering is as follows:

Assets	=	**Liabilities and Equity**
Financial Assets ↓ $500		Equity ↓ $650 (Income statement and RE)
		Financial liability ↑ $150

Available-for-sale (AFS)

This classification is only applied to financial assets and is used for non-derivative assets not falling into the other available headings. Despite the name, this does not imply the entity has any intention to sell the asset. This classification is most commonly applied to equity investments in traded companies.

Available-for-sale assets are recognised at fair value in the balance sheet. However, changes in the fair value of the asset are recognised **directly in equity without affecting the income statement**.

The cumulative gain or loss that was recognized in equity is recognized in the income statement when the available-for-sale financial asset is sold.

The logic behind the accounting here is that any gains or losses on the asset should only impact upon the income statement / profit and loss account once they have been realized (when the asset is sold).

Petro Inc

Petro purchases 2% of the equity of Greta Inc (a traded company) on 1 January for $800m.

Assets	=	Liabilities and Equity
Equity Investement ↑ $800m		
Cash ↓ $800m		

By the year end, the share price has fallen, and the equity investment has a fair value of $710m. The $90m loss is recognised directly in equity. This could be shown as a separate reserve or within retained earnings.

Assets	=	Liabilities and Equity
Equity Investment ↓ $90m		Equity ↓ $90m (Equity reserve account directly)

During the subsequent year, Petro disposes of its investment in Greta Inc at $814m. At this point the cumulative losses of $90m held in equity will be recognised in the income statement. This will have the impact of reducing the profit on disposal from $104m (814 - 710) to $14m. Note that this is the overall gain compared with the price paid (814 - 800). The accounting engineering is as follows:

Assets	=	Liabilities and Equity
Equity Investment ↓ $710m (value from the previous BS)		Equity ↑ $90m (The cumulative loss transferred to IS)
Cash ↑ $814m		Equity ↑ $14m (The profit net of the cumulative loss transferred to IS)

Note that if the investment was in shares of a non-trading company (and the fair value of the shares could therefore not be calculated), the equity investment would be *recorded at cost*.

Amortized cost accounting

Amortized cost accounting at the effective interest rate is used for all of the remaining classifications:

- Loan and receivable assets
- Held-to-maturity assets
- Other financial liabilities

Loans and receivables

This classification includes non-derivative financial assets:

- With fixed / determinable payments (i.e. not equities - AFS)
- Not quoted in an active market
- Not held for trading (i.e. not FV)

For short-term receivables, entities normally ignore effective interest. Receivables will therefore be shown at the amount expected to be received.

Held-to-maturity investments

This classification includes non-derivative financial assets:

- With fixed / determinable payments (i.e. not equities - AFS)
- Not loans or receivables
- Where the entity has the intention and ability to hold to maturity

This category is used for items such as traded bonds and money market instruments.

Other financial liabilities

This category will include items such as bond, loan and accounts payable liabilities.

As for receivables, entities normally ignore effective interest on short-term payables and show the amount due.

Under amortized cost accounting, the cash flows from a financial asset or liability are used to assess the effective interest rate (this will be the internal rate of return of the cash flows). Where significant (the instrument is sufficiently long-dated to make interest calculations significant), interest will be credited or charged on the asset or liability at the effective rate. This interest will add to the balance sheet value of the asset or liability, and will be charged or credited to the income statement / profit and loss account for the period. Any cash flows received or paid will reduce the value of asset or liability in the balance sheet.

Altrans Inc

Altrans Inc issues $100m nominal of 4-year 3% annual coupon bonds, receiving proceeds (net of issuance costs) of $83.44m. The effective interest rate is 8% (this represents the true cost of the financing and is calculated as the internal rate of return of the bond cash flows to the issuer). The bond is redeemed at par of $100m.

As was noted in the section on complex debt, the interest expense is calculated as:

Beginning debt amount * interest rate

Whereas the cash interest paid in the bond documentation is:

Par amount * coupon rate

We can use **BASE** analysis to generate the values needed for amortised cost accounting engineering.

	Year 1	Year 2	Year 3	Year 4
Beginning balance	83.44	87.11	91.08	95.37
Add - interest expense	6.68	6.97	7.29	7.63
Subtract - cash coupon and redemption paid	(3.00)	(3.00)	(3.00)	(103.00)
Ending balance	87.11	91.08	95.37	0.00

Refer back to the section on complex debt - accounting engineering for discounted bonds - for further detail on the accounting engineering entries.

Note that the same accounting technique is used for a loan issued or a bond asset being held. Namely,

- The item is recognised at net cost or proceeds
- Interest at the effective rate adds to the carrying value in the balance sheet and is recognised in the income statement
- Cash flows from the item will reduce the carrying amount of the item

Hedge accounting

Introduction

Almost all corporates will use derivatives to manage and hedge risks associated with their operations and financing. The hedge accounting rules aim to allow an entity to deviate from the normal accounting rules we have just seen for financial instruments in order reflect the economic reality of a hedged position.

The problem

Let us assume that a corporate has a loan on which it pays floating interest at LIBOR (the London interbank offered rate - a reference market interest rate). Our corporate wishes to have certainty regarding the cost of interest, and therefore hedges the loan with a pay fixed interest rate swap (this is a derivative contract under which the corporate will pay fixed interest and receive LIBOR on the amount of their loan - it effectively converts their interest exposure from floating to fixed interest).

Economically, our corporate now has certainty regarding their interest expense (since they are now paying fixed interest).

The rules for financial instruments require that all derivatives are accounted for at fair value through the income statement. Consequently, the interest rate swap will be adjusted for changes in fair value causing volatility in the income statement. The problem can be summarised as follows:

- Economically, the entity has no exposure to changing interest rates
- The Income statement will be volatile as interest rates change due to the marking to market of the interest rate swap

The solution

The hedge accounting rules allow modification of the treatment of the hedged item (the loan) or the hedging instrument (the interest rate swap). Where hedge accounting is applied, gains or losses on a hedging instrument are only recognized in the income statement at the same time as the hedged item will impact the income statement.

This means that where an entity has an effectively hedge in place, no income statement volatility will arise.

Hedging rules

The hedge accounting rules recognize four key risks that entities may hedge.

- Market price risk (the risk of the market price of a financial asset or commodity changing)
- Currency risk (the risk of a change in the value of a foreign-denominated cash flow or balance changing as the exchange rate varies)
- Interest rate risk (the risk of a change in an interest cash flow or value of a interest bearing instrument changing as the interest rate varies)
- Credit risk (the risk of a change in cash flows from or the value of a loan or bond changing due to the occurrence of a credit event such as default)

What items can be hedged?

The hedge accounting rules only permit hedging of:

- Financial assets and liabilities (not, therefore, physical items of inventory or PPE)
- A firm commitment or highly probable future transactions
- Net investment in foreign operations (including subsidiaries and associates / affiliates) for currency risk only

What can be used as a hedging instrument?

Risks must normally be hedged with a derivative contract with a third party (excluding written option contracts which will not hedge downside risk). Foreign denominated loans or deposits can also be used to hedge currency risk.

What is an effective hedge?

In order for an entity to apply hedge accounting, they must document the intended hedge and must be able to demonstrate that:

- The hedge is anticipated to be effective
- The hedge is shown to be retrospectively effective

In order to define a hedge as effective, the change in the value of the hedging instrument must fall within the range 80% – 125% of the change in the value of the hedged item.

Types of hedge

There are three types of hedge relationship, with broadly two accounting treatments:

- Fair value hedge
- Cash flow hedge
- Net investment hedge

Fair value hedge

This is a hedge of the value of a recognized asset or liability or a firm commitment (in practice, firm commitments are normally accounted for as cash flow hedges).

Assuming the hedging instrument is a derivative, it would normally be accounted for at fair value through the income statement. However, if the hedged item is accounted for under amortized cost, it will not be adjusted to fair value. This will cause balance sheet volatility despite the value being hedged. Even if the item were accounted for as available-for-sale, only the changes in the derivative fair value will be recognized in the income statement, causing income statement volatility.

Hedge accounting engineering

In order to ensure there is no balance sheet or income statement volatility, the accounting for the **hedged item** is modified to replicate the accounting for the derivative - namely it is accounted for at *fair value through the income statement.*

Below are some examples of possible fair value hedges. The first is widely used by corporates.

Hedged risk	Hedged item	Hedging instrument
Interest rate risk	*Fixed interest* loans, bonds and deposits	Interest rate swaps and forward rate agreements (FRAs)
Currency risk	Forecast foreign denominated purchases and sales	Currency forwards, futures and options
Equity price risk	Traded equity with reliable fair value	Equity forward or option

Huxley Corp

Huxley Corp has issued fixed coupon bonds at par ($1,000). Huxley simultaneously enters a receive fixed (pay LIBOR) swap. The swap has a **zero** fair value at initiation. The swap is anticipated to have a fair value which changes by approximately the same amount as the bonds, but in the opposite direction.

Assets	=	Liabilities and Equity
Cash ↑ $1,000		Bond liability ↑ $1,000

At the subsequent year end the fair value of the bonds has increased to $1,130. The swap has a positive fair value (derivative asset) of $122.

Was the hedge effective?

The hedge effectiveness can be calculated as:

$$\frac{\text{Change in FV of hedging instrument}}{\text{Change in FV of hedged item}} = \frac{0 - 122}{1,000 - 1,130} = \boldsymbol{94\%}$$

Since the hedge has been effective, the accounting treatment of the bonds may be modified to fair value through the income statement to match the derivative.

Assets	=	Liabilities and Equity
Derivative asset ↑ $122 (The swap is adjusted to FV)		Equity ↑ $122 (Income statement and RE)
		Bond liability ↑ $130 (The bond is adjusted to FV)
		Equity ↓ $130 (Income statement and RE)

Notice that there will be **some** balance sheet and income statement volatility since the hedge was not perfect. Volatility and earnings impact is restricted, however, to hedge ineffectiveness of $8 (130 - 122).

Cash flow hedge

This is a hedge of changes in the value of an expected or forecast future **cash flow**.

Given that the cash flow is yet to occur, it will not be recorded. However, the derivative contract will be entered into in advance, and recorded at fair value through the income statement. This will result in income statement and balance sheet volatility.

Hedge accounting engineering

In order to ensure there is no balance sheet or income statement volatility, the accounting for the **hedging instrument** is modified - gains and losses arising on the derivative will be taken **directly to equity** (to the extent that it matches the change in fair value of the cash flow) rather than the income statement. Where the change in value of the derivative exceeds the change in value of the cash flow, any excess will be taken to the income statement.

When the future cash flow has an income statement impact, the gains and losses on the derivative that have been held in equity are transferred (or "recycled") through the income statement.

Below are some examples of possible cash flow hedges. Cash flow hedges are more common than fair value hedges in practice.

Hedged risk	Hedged item	Hedging instrument
Interest rate risk	*Fixed interest* loans, bonds and deposits	Interest rate swaps and forward rate agreements (FRAs)
Currency risk	Forecast foreign denominated purchases and sales	Currency forwards, futures and options
Commodity price risk	Forecast purchase or sale of a commodity	Commodity future, forward or option

Clara SA

Clara SA negotiates a supply of copper from a local supplier. The copper is required for a production run of copper tubing starting after the year end. Based on current supplier prices, the cash flow has a fair value of $550. The supplier will establish a price for the copper at the time of delivery, depending on market prices for copper at that time.

In order to eliminate exposure to changes in the copper price, Clara SA enters a forward contract to buy the required copper. The forward contract has a zero fair value at inception (no accounting entries are required as the copper purchase has not taken place, and the derivative has a zero far value).

At the year end, the future cash flow has fallen in value to $490 (due to a decline in copper prices). The forward contract now has a negative fair value (derivative liability) of $68.

Hedge effectiveness

The hedge effectiveness can be calculated as:

$$\frac{\text{Change in FV of hedging instrument}}{\text{Change in FV of hedged item}} = \frac{0 - \text{-}68}{550 - 490} = \textit{113\%}$$

The hedge has been effective. However, since the change in the value of the derivative exceeds the change in the value of the cash flow, the excess movement in the derivative fair value ($8) will be taken through the income statement. The majority of the movement ($60) will be taken directly to equity.

Assets	=	Liabilities and Equity
		Derivative liability ↑ $68 (The derivative is adjusted to FV)
		Equity ↓ $60 (Cash flow hedging reserve)
		Equity ↓ $8 (Income statement and RE)

There is *some* balance sheet and income statement volatility since the hedge was not perfect. Volatility is restricted, however, to hedge ineffectiveness.

By the time Clara SA is ready to purchase the copper, prices have risen and the cash cost is $560. The derivative now has a fair value of positive $11 (derivative asset).

Cumulative hedge effectiveness

The hedge effectiveness can be calculated on a cumulative basis as:

$$\frac{\text{Change in FV of hedging instrument}}{\text{Change in FV of hedged item}} = \frac{11 - 0}{560 - 550} = \textbf{\textit{110\%}}$$

Effectiveness for the period was:

$$\frac{\text{Change in FV of hedging instrument}}{\text{Change in FV of hedged item}} = \frac{-68 - 11}{490 - 560} = \textbf{\textit{113\%}}$$

The excess change in the value of the derivative (79 - 70 = 9) is taken through the income statement, with $70 taken directly to equity.

Assets	=	Liabilities and Equity
Derivative asset ↑ $11 (The derivative is adjusted to FV)		Derivative liability ↓ $68 (The derivative is adjusted to FV)
		Equity ↑ $70 (Cash flow hedging reserve)
		Equity ↑ $9 (Income statement and RE)

Recycling gains through the income statement

Once the copper has been purchased, it will appear in inventory at the price paid of $560 (cash down, inventory up). Let us assume the copper forward is cash settled and removed (cash up $11, derivative asset down $11).

When the copper tubing is sold, the hedged cash flow ($560 paid for the copper) will enter the income statement as cost of goods sold. The cumulative gain on the derivative held in equity (cash flow hedging reserve down $60 then up $70 = net $10) is now transferred to the income statement to match the hedged cash flow.

Assets	=	**Liabilities and Equity**
Inventory ⬇ $560 (Transferred to the IS)		Equity ⬇ $560 (Cost of goods sold in IS and RE)
		Equity ⬇ $10 (Net gain removed from cash flow hedging reserve)
		Equity ⬆ $10 (Recycled to the IS - cost of goods sold - and RE)

Note that the gains or losses on the hedge are recycled through the income statement at the same time and in the same place (cost of goods sold) as the hedged cash flow.

Net investment hedge

A net investment hedge is a hedge of currency risk associated with the foreign-denominated net assets (including any applicable goodwill) of foreign operations, equity method investments and subsidiaries.

A net investment hedge may be executed with derivatives (such as currency forwards or swaps) or with a foreign denominated loan.

Under normal accounting rules, the currency gains and losses on the foreign investment will be taken *directly to equity* (and recycled through the income statement if the foreign investment is sold). However, currency gains and losses on derivative contracts or foreign denominated loans will be *recognized in the income statement*, causing income statement volatility despite the hedge.

Hedge accounting engineering

A net investment hedge is accounted for just like a cash flow hedge - the accounting for the *hedging instrument* is modified to match the accounting for the currency gains and losses on the foreign investment - gains and losses arising on the derivative will be taken *directly to equity* rather than the income statement.

If the foreign investment is sold, the currency gains and losses on the hedging instrument and the foreign operations are both recycled through the income statement together.

Just as for the other hedges, income statement volatility will be restricted to hedge ineffectiveness.

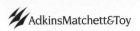